Russell GRANT'S

ASTRO-DIARY

With colour almanac

1995

LIBRA

B▦XTREE

STOP PRESS!

VISIT THE MAGNIFICENT PYRAMIDS IN EGYPT

▲▲▲

WIN A FABULOUS 7 DAY HOLIDAY FOR 2 TO GIZA AND VISIT THE MAGICAL PYRAMIDS!

See last page of this book for full details.

First published in Great Britain in 1994 by Boxtree Limited,
Broadwall House,
21 Broadwall, London SE1 9PL

Copyright © 1994 Russell Grant

10 9 8 7 6 5 4 3 2 1

ISBN: 0 7522 0932 9

Phototypeset by The Creative Centre.

Printed and bound in Great Britain by Cox and Wyman Ltd, Reading.

A CIP catalogue entry for this book is available from the British Library.

Cover design by Head Design.

Cover photography by Mark Lawrence.

INTRODUCTION

Hello my friends,

So many of you have written to tell me just how much my year ahead books have meant to you. You say they have given you the guidance you needed to make the most of your coming annums.

But you also said you wanted something more – a compact and handy book that you could carry around with you at all times and have something to consult any time, any place, any where at a moment's notice. In fact many of you have specifically asked for your own astrological diary.

Well here it is! My new zodiac diary exclusively prepared for you. Where you can get your very own sun sign day-by-day forecast at a moment's notice AND have the space to put in those special days, important appointments and juicy secrets.

Your own personal and private journal packed with starry information; a confidential diary that is for your eyes only!

I am sure that you will like what my pals at Boxtree and I have put together because I just know you are going to find your Astro-Diary an invaluable wee friend and ally to help you make the most of 1995. I am sure it will become an essential adviser and invaluable helper in your everyday life and busy world.

In the meantime I hope your Astro-Dairy will be full of happy dates, gay celebrations and joyful events all year long starting from January 1st right through to December 31st.

And don't forget if you have anything you want to ask just drop me a line as I'm always happy to hear from a friend.

Lots of Love,
Russell.

SUNDAY 30th October — St Serapion of Antioch

LOVE: It's a gay day for spending your Sabbath in the loving way!
LOOT: A delectable time for spending loot on luxury and finery.
LIFE: A thing of beauty is a joy forever this fine Sunday.
LUCK: ☾☾☾

A. M: *P. M:*

Born: Henry Winkler, 1945, US actor
Event: Scottish Caledonian Canal opened, 1822

MONDAY 31st October — St Wolfgang

LOVE: There's nothing spooky about your love life this Hallowe'en.
LOOT: A major purchase is on the horizon so get your funds in place.
LIFE: If you have to entertain people in business do it socially today.
LUCK: ☾☾☾

A. M: *P. M:*

Born: John Keats, 1795, poet
Event: Disney's film of '*Dumbo*' released, 1941

TUESDAY 1st November — All Saints

LOVE: Love will find a way as it won't get lost with you around.
LOOT: You're on your marks to make a mint of money very soon.
LIFE: Be active and decisive, don't let the grass grow under your feet.
LUCK: ☾☾

A. M: *P. M:*

Born: Gary Player, 1935, golfer
Event: First Premium Bonds sold, 1956

WEDNESDAY 2nd November — St Eustace

LOVE: Falling in love now will mean a lifetime of total happiness.
LOOT: Everything in your financial garden is blooming rosy now!
LIFE: This is one of the nicest days ever; make it work for you.
LUCK: ☾☾☾☾☾

A. M: *P. M:*

Born: Marie Antoinette, 1755, Queen of Louis XVI
Event: Channel Four goes on the air, 1982

THURSDAY 3rd November

St Hubert

LOVE: Someone has plans for you and it could include the boudoir!
LOOT: A prize possession will soon be yours. Make your plans now.
LIFE: Good news is coming from a hidden source or admirer.
LUCK: ☺☺☺☺

A. M: *P. M:*

Born: Charles Bronson, 1922, actor
Event: First dog in space,1957

FRIDAY 4th November

St Charles Borromeo

LOVE: An unusual person takes your fancy, but will it be a lasting love?
LOOT: You can't afford to rely on anyone and that includes computers.
LIFE: Disorganisation could mean a lost opportunity, so get tidy!
LUCK: ☺☺☺

A. M: *P. M:*

Born: Lena Zavaroni, 1964, singer
Event: Nelson's Column in Trafalgar Square finished, 1843

SATURDAY 5th November

St Elizabeth

LOVE: If you're expecting a golden shower of amour today, forget it.
LOOT: Bills, demands, debts, you name it this red letter day.
LIFE: Problems with authority could have you giving them a rocket.
LUCK: ☺☺

A. M: *P. M:*

Born: Lester Piggott 1935, champion jockey
Event: Richard Nixon elected US President, 1968

NOTES:

Thursday 3rd November
Eclipsed New Moon in Scorpio

NOVEMBER						
S	M	T	W	T	F	S
		1	2	3	4	5
6	7	8	9	10	11	12
13	14	15	16	17	18	19
20	21	22	23	24	25	26
27	28	29	30			

SUNDAY 6th November — St Illtyd

LOVE: If you fancy someone special, then for goodness sake tell 'em.
LOOT: Transactions and negotiations can be concluded today.
LIFE: An excellent day for getting to know folk and keeping in touch.
LUCK: ♘♘

A. M: P. M:

Born: Adolphe Sax, 1814, inventor of saxophone
Event: First H-bomb exploded in Pacific, 1952

MONDAY 7th November — St Willibrord

LOVE: The generation gap shows romantically, but who's telling!
LOOT: Keep your options open and you'll end up all the more richer.
LIFE: An extraordinary day with extraordinary happenings - fab!
LUCK: ♘♘♘♘

A. M: P. M:

Born: Joni Mitchell, 1943, singer
Event: Russian Revolution started, 1917

TUESDAY 8th November — St Willehad

LOVE: Plan something a little bit special to hook your sweetheart.
LOOT: A disappointment is possible when a plan or idea falls down.
LIFE: Apart from ignoring gossip much of the day has a good outlook.
LUCK: ♘♘

A. M: P. M:

Born: Ken Dodd, 1931, comedian
Event: Yeti footprints discovered in the Himalayas, 1951

WEDNESDAY 9th November — St Simeon Metaphrastes

LOVE: There's something about you that brings out the best in people.
LOOT: A financial loss however small is possible due to a silly whim.
LIFE: Envy and jealousy aren't very nice, but it's all around you now.
LUCK: ♘

A. M: P. M:

Born: Edward VII, 1841
Event: Kaiser Bill abdicated to Holland, 1918

THURSDAY 10th November   St Justus

LOVE: You could jump out of the frying pan into the fire over a lover.
LOOT: A splendid period for buying, selling, wheeling and dealing.
LIFE: Stand back and think or you'll rue the day you acted in haste.
LUCK: U

A. M: P. M:

Born: Robert Carrier, 1944, gourmet chef
Event: Hirohito becomes Emperor of Japan, 1928

FRIDAY 11th November   St Martin of Tours

LOVE: A very special day for lovers, especially if you're tying the knot.
LOOT: Business and money matters initiated now bring long term profits.
LIFE: Fidelity is what separates you from the rest. Happiness is certain.
LUCK: UUUU

A. M: P. M:

Born: Doestoevsky, 1821, writer
Event: First air-balloon crossing of the Alps, 1906

SATURDAY 12th November   St Benedict

LOVE: When will someone learn that it's love you want not lust.
LOOT: Act the tortoise rather than the hare and you'll get somewhere.
LIFE: Be warned of callous folk who have no thought for you.
LUCK: UU

A. M: P. M:

Born: Stephanie Powers, 1943, US actress
Event: Chloroform used as an anaesthetic, 1847

NOTES:

NOVEMBER						
S	M	T	W	T	F	S
		1	2	3	4	5
6	7	8	9	10	11	12
13	14	15	16	17	18	19
20	21	22	23	24	25	26
27	28	29	30			

NOVEMBER 1994

SUNDAY 13th November — St Abbo

LOVE: The rose of romance blooms in all its loving splendour now.
LOOT: Money poured into anything artistic will reap rich rewards.
LIFE: Put your feelings down on paper and watch them reciprocated.
LUCK: ☉☉☉☉

A. M: P. M:

Born: Augustine of Hippo, AD345
Event: Cyclones and flooding kill over half million in Pakistan, 1970

MONDAY 14th November — St Dubricius

LOVE: You're not at your most demonstrative today, so stick to work.
LOOT: Being astute commercially will put you in line for success.
LIFE: When it comes to business acumen there's no-one quite like you.
LUCK: ☉☉

A. M: P. M:

Born: King Hussein of Jordan, 1935
Event: Coventry Cathedral bombed, 1940

TUESDAY 15th November — St Albert the Great

LOVE: Electric! That's how it is when you meet someone very soon.
LOOT: Alternative avenues are the routes to take to get rich quick.
LIFE: Be open to suggestion and ready to fly off at a moment's notice.
LUCK: ☉☉☉☉

A. M: P. M:

Born: Petula Clark, 1934, singer
Event: First ever news broadcast by the BBC, 1922

WEDNESDAY 16th November — St Edmund of Abingdon

LOVE: Don't believe all you hear, but check it out before you disregard it.
LOOT: Get a second opinion before you throw good money after bad.
LIFE: Someone's being very crafty and hoping to sidetrack you.
LUCK: ☉

A. M: P. M:

Born: Griff Rhys Jones, 1953, comedian
Event: Suez Canal opened, 1869

THURSDAY *17th November*   St Elizabeth of Abingdon

LOVE: You've so much going for you, you're irresistible now.
LOOT: Optimise your financial opportunities by following a global link.
LIFE: If you can travel far across the seas you'll make your fortune.
LUCK: ʊʊʊʊ

A. M: *P. M:*

Born: Jonathan Ross, 1960, broadcaster
Event: '*Godspell*' first performance in London, 1971

FRIDAY *18th November*   St Odo

LOVE: There's something not quite right about today; you're confused.
LOOT: It's the end of the road for a cash agreement or partnership.
LIFE: Can you trust to your feelings at the moment? I think not Sweetie.
LUCK: ʊʊ

A. M: *P. M:*

Born: Gallup poll man George Gallup, 1901
Event: Big Ben bell was struck for the first time, 1858

SATURDAY *19th November*   St Mechthild

LOVE: Problems arise over a love match due to a difficult parent.
LOOT: A less than charming autocrat makes totally unreasonable demands.
LIFE: However much you try to please folk today you won't succeed.
LUCK: ʊ

A. M: *P. M:*

Born: Indira Gandhi, 1917, Indian stateswoman
Event: Abraham Lincoln's Gettysburg Address, 1863

NOTES:

Friday 18th November
Full Moon in Taurus

NOVEMBER						
S	M	T	W	T	F	S
		1	2	3	4	5
6	7	8	9	10	11	12
13	14	15	16	17	18	19
20	21	22	23	24	25	26
27	28	29	30			

SUNDAY 20th November — St Edmund the Martyr

LOVE: There's a lot of steamy passion around now - you're hot stuff!
LOOT: It's not what you know but who you know that matters most now.
LIFE: You're in line for a position of great power. Fate is your friend.
LUCK: ☾☾☾

A. M: *P. M:*

Born: Alistair Cooke, 1908, broadcaster
Event: Snowdonia becomes a National Park, 1951

MONDAY 21st November — St Gelasius

LOVE: A gentle day full of tender moments so do what you can to please.
LOOT: Flutter your eyelashes, pout your lips, and you're in the money!
LIFE: Charming and calculating are your trademarks now. Use them well.
LUCK: ☾☾

A. M: *P. M:*

Born: René Magritte, 1898, artist
Event: Parliamentary proceedings televised first time, 1989

TUESDAY 22nd November — St Cecillia

LOVE: With such a stunning silver tongue, who can resist you now?
LOOT: Put yourself about a bit and start networking and cash will come.
LIFE: Communicate and make contact and the better your prospects will be.
LUCK: ☾☾☾☾

A. M: *P. M:*

Born: Charles de Gaulle, 1890, French President
Event: Margaret Thatcher resigns as PM, 1990

WEDNESDAY 23rd November — St Amphilochius

LOVE: Venus starts to move forward and your affairs of the heart prosper.
LOOT: Your whole financial situation is about to become more profitable.
LIFE: What you need is a jolly good night out with a meal thrown in!
LUCK: ☾☾☾

A. M: *P. M:*

Born: Billy the Kid, 1859, outlaw
Event: *Doctor Who* broadcast for first time, 1963

THURSDAY 24th November — St Chrysogonus

LOVE: Don't ignore someone's fond feelings for you, they really mean it.
LOOT: Spend some lolly on beautifying your surroundings. That's nice!
LIFE: A journey, perhaps over or by water, could lead you to your destiny.
LUCK: ☻☻☻

A. M: P. M:

Born: Ian Botham, 1955, cricketer
Event: Lee Harvey Oswald shot dead, 1963

FRIDAY 25th November — St Clement I

LOVE: You're not really sure what someone means to you. Give it time.
LOOT: Steer clear of cash commitment or the interest will cripple you.
LIFE: A variety of difficulties doesn't make this the most auspicious
        Friday.
LUCK: ☻☻

A. M: P. M:

Born: Joe di Maggio, 1914, boxer
Event: *Do They Know It's Christmas* recorded, 1984

SATURDAY 26th November — St Siricius

LOVE: Who is the last person in the world you thought you'd fancy?
        Well.....
LOOT: Got plans for your cash? Well I bet they alter 100 per cent after
        today.
LIFE: Something totally unforeseen plops from the heavens to surprise
        you.
LUCK: ☻☻☻
A. M: P. M:
Born: *Peanuts* cartoonist Charles Schultz, 1922
Event: Tutankhamun Tomb opened in Luxor, 1922

NOTES:

NOVEMBER						
S	M	T	W	T	F	S
		1	2	3	4	5
6	7	8	9	10	11	12
13	14	15	16	17	18	19
20	21	22	23	24	25	26
27	28	29	30			

SUNDAY 27th November — St Virgil

LOVE: A right clodhopper of a lover will annoy you something chronic!
LOOT: There's a lot of fool's gold around today, make sure it's not yours.
LIFE: A child or man will be the main reason for a loss of your temper.
LUCK: U

A. M: *P. M:*

Born: Jimi Hendrix, 1942, musician
Event: French Fleet sunk at Toulon, 1942

MONDAY 28th November — St James

LOVE: There's no such thing as love today, so just forget it exists.
LOOT: Even hard work seems to bring scant reward - hang on in there.
LIFE: Life is such heavy-going but don't give up, it will get better.
LUCK: U

A. M: *P. M:*

Born: William Blake, 1757, poet and painter
Event: Royal Society founded, 1660

TUESDAY 29th November — St Cuthbert Mayne

LOVE: A secret admirer or clandestine liaison makes amour *tres* interesting!
LOOT: When it comes to intuition yours is piercingly accurate over money now.
LIFE: You're best to bow to someone's better judgment rather than ignore it.
LUCK: UU
A. M: *P. M:*
Born: Derek Jameson, 1929, broadcaster
Event: First day of '999' phone number direct to Scotland Yard, 1937

WEDNESDAY 30th November — St Andrew

LOVE: Choose a Christmas card that expresses your feelings precisely.
LOOT: It's amazing how your social life can be a passport to making money.
LIFE: Invitations, phone calls and a general hubbub brightens up your life.
LUCK: UUU

A. M: *P. M:*

Born: Jonathan Swift, 1667, writer
Event: Crystal Palace, London, destroyed in fire, 1936

THURSDAY *1st December*   St Eligius

LOVE: There's a strange sensation around you now - could it be love?
LOOT: Consider buying a Christmas gift that means more than just money.
LIFE: You're lost in a dreamworld today, and boy isn't it just dandy!
LUCK: ∪∪

A. M: *P. M:*

Born: Madame Tussaud, 1761
Event: Potato introduced by Drake, 1586

FRIDAY *2nd December*   St Chromatius

LOVE: Feelings are so intense today, it's bound to end in a love sexy Friday.
LOOT: Just because you can't see something, doesn't mean it's not happening.
LIFE: Kismet combines with Providence to ensure a future that's pure gold.
LUCK: ∪∪∪∪

A. M: *P. M:*
Born:Julie Harris, 1925, US film actress
Event:Gillette patents first safety razor, 1901

SATURDAY *3rd December*   St Francis Xavier

LOVE: Rest easy lovewise. You need time to think and consider your own self.
LOOT: Second thoughts never hurt anyone. Have three or four if necessary.
LIFE: A welcome chance has come to stand and stare. Do nothing yet.
LUCK: ∪

A. M: *P. M:*

Born: Mel Smith, 1952, comedian
Event: Worst plane crash in Canaries, 1972

NOTES:

Friday 2nd December
New Moon in Sagittarius

DECEMBER						
S	M	T	W	T	F	S
				1	2	3
4	5	6	7	8	9	10
11	12	13	14	15	16	17
18	19	20	21	22	23	24
25	26	27	28	29	30	31

SUNDAY 4th December St Barbara

LOVE: It's not like you to be so unfeeling - but that's how it is now.
LOOT: A cool warning comes to make it a frugal Yule - budget your gifts.
LIFE: You feel unappreciated and unwanted - self pity isn't your scene.
LUCK: ∪

A. M: *P. M:*

Born: Edith Cavell, 1865, nurse
Event: Smog killed over 60 people in London, 1962

MONDAY 5th December St Clement of Alexandria

LOVE: You might receive something that will really set you thinking.
LOOT: Get down Santa's grotto and enjoy a second childhood today.
LIFE: In a quandary? Well that's nothing compared to someone else.
LUCK: ∪∪

A. M: *P. M:*

Born: General Custer, 1839, US cavalry commander
Event: Britain's first motorway, the Preston Bypass, opened 1958

TUESDAY 6th December St Nicholas

LOVE: St. Nicholas' Day leaves you a little concerned about amour.
LOOT: There's a chance coming soon that'll fill your coffers to the brim.
LIFE: An office or company event will leave you with a secret to keep.
LUCK: ∪∪

A. M: *P. M:*

Born: Jonathan King, 1944, broadcaster
Event: Bangladesh became Independent, 1971

WEDNESDAY 7th December St Ambrose

LOVE: Jealousy is rampant in either you or a loved one now.
LOOT: Don't take on any loans or the like with strings attached.
LIFE: Be warned of a man who is very manipulative around you.
LUCK: ∪

A. M: *P. M:*

Born: Eli Wallach, 1915, US actor
Event: Attack on Pearl Harbour, 1941

THURSDAY 8th December   St Patapius

LOVE: The course of true love runs oh so very smooth today.
LOOT: A very profitable time to invest in long term fiscal schemes.
LIFE: An older person dispenses very wise advice, be sure to take it.
LUCK: ☺☺☺

A. M: *P. M:*

Born: Mary Queen of Scots, 1542
Event: John Lennon murdered in New York, 1980

FRIDAY 9th December   St Budoc

LOVE: It's time to tell someone how you really feel - so go ahead now.
LOOT: Implement a vision or notion this year and you'll boost your
          boodle.
LIFE: Wanderlust governs your thoughts, you want to travel the world.
LUCK: ☺☺☺☺

A. M: *P. M:*

Born: Frozen food pioneer Clarence Birdseye, 1886
Event: First episode of *Coronation Street* broadcast, 1960

SATURDAY 10th December   St Miltiades

LOVE: Take some time off to select a present that describes your feelings.
LOOT: A fairly good day for earning or purchasing, so it's either/or!
LIFE: The last thing you want now is to be stuck in a rut - are you?
LUCK: ☺☺☺

A. M: *P. M:*

Born: Dorothy Lamour, 1914, US singer/actress
Event: First Nobel Prizes, 1901

NOTES:

DECEMBER						
S	M	T	W	T	F	S
				1	2	3
4	5	6	7	8	9	10
11	12	13	14	15	16	17
18	19	20	21	22	23	24
25	26	27	28	29	30	31

SUNDAY 11th December   St Damasus

LOVE: Don't push a partner or ask for a decision on anything now.
LOOT: Keep a hold of your dosh and don't let it out of your sight!
LIFE: Busy doing nothing? Well that's just how your life should be.
LUCK: ☽

A. M: *P. M:*

Born: Alexander Solzhenitsyn, 1918, writer
Event: Concorde prototype first shown in Toulouse, 1967

MONDAY 12th December   St Alexander

LOVE: There's someone lurking in your life who has designs on you....
LOOT: An act of charity or fund raising will enhance your reputation.
LIFE: Watch out for a man who might not be all he seems.
LUCK: ☽

A. M: *P. M:*

Born: Jasper Conran, 1959, fashion designer
Event: First women members elected to the Jockey Club, 1977

TUESDAY 13th December   St Lucy

LOVE: Grab that mistletoe and carry it around with you all day long!
LOOT: Talk with people who know about money before doing anything.
LIFE: Be practical and logical and your life will take a turn for the best.
LUCK: ☽☽

A. M: *P. M:*

Born: The Aga Khan, 1936
Event: Tasman discovered New Zealand, 1642

WEDNESDAY 14th December   St John of the Cross

LOVE: If you haven't sent a card to your amour then get it in the post now!
LOOT: An excellent chance for completing plans ready for a new year
       launch.
LIFE: News comes in from north, south, east and west. My you're
       popular!
LUCK: ☽☽☽

A. M: *P. M:*
Born: Nostradamus, 1503, astrologer
Event: Norwegian explorer, Amundsen, first person to reach South Pole, 1911

THURSDAY 15th December   St Mary di Rosa

LOVE: Be soft, gentle and romantic rather than a randy, unfeeling so-and-so.
LOOT: There's wonga you win and loot you lose this mixed monetary day.
LIFE: Someone hasn't a clue how to handle you; they go about it all wrong.
LUCK: ∪∪

A. M: *P. M:*

Born: Jean Paul Getty, 1892, industrialist
Event: Piccadilly Line underground opened, 1906

FRIDAY 16th December   St Eusebius

LOVE: A sweetheart has plans for you, but don't jump the gun and spoil it.
LOOT: Be rash with your cash and it will be a waste of your year-long
        efforts.
LIFE: If you're off travelling soon then you're gonna have a lorra fun.
LUCK: ∪∪

A. M: *P. M:*

Born: Jane Austen, 1775, writer
Event: Glenn Miller's plane lost without trace, body never recovered, 1944

SATURDAY 17th December   St Begga

LOVE: Let your other half do all the running whilst you take a breather.
LOOT: Money won't have the desired effect by spending it, so save it!
LIFE: Take a pause and study your future - ready for action in 1995?
LUCK: ∪

A. M: *P. M:*

Born: Tommy Steele, 1936, entertainer
Event: Francis Drake left for round the world trip from Plymouth, 1577

NOTES:

DECEMBER						
S	M	T	W	T	F	S
				1	2	3
4	5	6	7	8	9	10
11	12	13	14	15	16	17
18	19	20	21	22	23	24
25	26	27	28	29	30	31

SUNDAY 18th December — St Frumentius

LOVE: The Full Moon makes someone ardent and avid this Noel.
LOOT: Never a lender nor borrower be, even if it's a relative.
LIFE: Moves and changes are likely in your surroundings now.
LUCK: ☾☾☾

A. M: P. M:

Born: Steven Spielberg, 1947, US film director
Event: Death penalty for murder abolished, 1969

MONDAY 19th December — St Anastasius I of Antioch

LOVE: It's a lovely day for being with the one person you adore.
LOOT: If you want to lash out your loot then spend it on the home.
LIFE: A family reunion or a visit from your kith and kin is likely.
LUCK: ☾☾☾

A. M: P. M:

Born: Edith Piaf, 1915, French singer
Event: First emergency ambulance service in London, 1905

TUESDAY 20th December — St Ignatius of Antioch

LOVE: Don't peg back your feelings, it's all or nothing with you now.
LOOT: You're about to receive something you've always wanted.....
LIFE: Split second news and last minute action is called for today.
LUCK: ☾☾☾

A. M: P. M:

Born: Bo Derek, 1957, US actress
Event: Atomic ice-breaker, "Lenin", first began operating, 1959

WEDNESDAY 21st December — St Peter Canisius

LOVE: Fun and laughter ring around your heart as love envelops you.
LOOT: Last minute gifts could cost a packet, so be more organised.
LIFE: Pack your bags and get ready to be off to the sun or snow.
LUCK: ☾☾☾

A. M: P. M:

Born: Chris Evert, 1954, tennis champion
Event: The Pilgrim Fathers landed in the New World, 1620

THURSDAY 22nd December   St Anastasia

LOVE: The Solstice brings a touch of envy - whose green eye is it?
LOOT: Family matters dominate so pour any spare loot into the home.
LIFE: A most important domestic period starts from this moment on.
LUCK: ☋

A. M: *P. M:*

Born: Noel Edmonds, 1948, TV presenter
Event: Lockerbie terrorist bomb disaster, 1988

FRIDAY 23rd December   St John of Kanty

LOVE: People blow hot and cold today, just make sure it's not you.
LOOT: The Christmas spirit should be spent on practical pressies.
LIFE: Stick to commercial and business matters - tie up loose ends.
LUCK: ☋☋

A. M: *P. M:*

Born: Queen Silvia of Sweden, 1943
Event: Aldwych Theatre opened in London, 1905

SATURDAY 24th December   St Adela

LOVE: Talk about sexy! Well why talk about it? Get down to it darling.
LOOT: Enjoy yourself as much as you like slogging it around the shops.
LIFE: You feel like the fairy on top of the Christmas tree - lucky you.
LUCK: ☋☋☋☋

A. M: *P. M:*

Born: Matthew Arnold, 1822, poet
Event: Apollo VIII astronaut reads Bible from moon's orbit, 1968

NOTES:

Sunday 18th December
Full Moon in Gemini

DECEMBER						
S	M	T	W	T	F	S
					1	2	3
4	5	6	7	8	9	10
11	12	13	14	15	16	17
18	19	20	21	22	23	24
25	26	27	28	29	30	31

SUNDAY 25th December   St Alburga

LOVE: There's something very unusual but interesting this Yule.
LOOT: Don't judge everything by how much it costs my dear.
LIFE: Glad tidings and merry moments make it a jolly old day.
LUCK: ℧℧℧

A. M: *P. M:*

Born: Annie Lennox, 1954, singer
Event: Captain Cook discovers Christmas Island, 1777

MONDAY 26th December   St Stephen

LOVE: You want to wring someone's neck they're so rude.
LOOT: Scurrilous lies about cash mean you lose faith or trust.
LIFE: Boxing Day? A kid tries your patience so much it will be!
LUCK: ℧

A. M: *P. M:*

Born: Mao Tse-Tung, 1893, Chinese leader
Event: The Curies discover Radium, 1898

TUESDAY 27th December   St John

LOVE: Don't take what anyone says to heart, they're confused.
LOOT: Someone will move the goal posts when it comes to cash.
LIFE: A difficult day if you want to get sense out of anyone.
LUCK: ℧

A. M: *P. M:*

Born: Janet Street-Porter, 1946, producer
Event: Darwin set sail on HMS Beagle, 1869

WEDNESDAY 28th December   St Anthony of Lerins

LOVE: You might score elsewhere but it won't be in romance.
LOOT: Count up your assets to know where you stand come '95.
LIFE: Put your energy wholeheartedly into work or business plans.
LUCK: ℧℧

A. M: *P. M:*

Born: Nigel Kennedy, 1956, violinist
Event: Chewing gum patented in the States, 1869

THURSDAY 29th December — St Thomas à Becket

LOVE: Hogmanay's drawing closer as does someone to your heart.
LOOT: Do some costings and set yourself a budget for 1995 now.
LIFE: A perfect day for making your resolutions for the New Year.
LUCK: ♡♡♡

A. M: P. M:

Born: Marianne Faithful, 1946, singer
Event: Thomas à Becket murdered, 1170

FRIDAY 30th December — St Anysia

LOVE: St. Valentine pops in a little early to pluck your heartstrings.
LOOT: Be imaginative with your money and you'll be quids in.
LIFE: The run up to the New Year has never been so romantic for you.
LUCK: ♡♡♡♡

A. M: P. M:

Born: Rudyard Kipling, 1865, writer
Event: First performance of *Pirates of Penzance*, 1879

SATURDAY 31st December — St Sylvester

LOVE: You'll hug, kiss or squeeze anyone tonight, you're not choosy!
LOOT: Any Libra who hesitates is lost when it comes to loot today.
LIFE: Be ready to leap into 1995 with all guns blazing - go get 'em!
LUCK: ♡♡♡

A. M: P. M:

Born: Donna Summer, 1948, US singer
Event: Closure of notorious Newgate Gaol, 1881

NOTES:

DECEMBER

S	M	T	W	T	F	S
				1	2	3
4	5	6	7	8	9	10
11	12	13	14	15	16	17
18	19	20	21	22	23	24
25	26	27	28	29	30	31

SUNDAY *1st January* *New Year's Day*   St Basil

LOVE: Home is where the heart is – so prove it to kith and kin.
LOOT: Spend wisely but well on improving your abode.
LIFE: Any career connected with the abode will do well now.
LUCK: ☋

A. M: *P. M:*

Born: Joe Orton, 1933, playwright
Event: UK, Irish Republic & Denmark joined EEC, 1973

MONDAY *2nd January*   St Macarius of Alexandria

LOVE: You'll meet someone who dazzles you with their charms.
LOOT: You'll spot something in a shop – but will you still like it when you
            get home?
LIFE: A colleague will be protective and kind.
LUCK: ☋

A. M: *P. M:*

Born: David Bailey, 1938, Photographer
Event: Russian rocket, Luna 1, launched, first rocket to pass by the moon, 1959

TUESDAY *3rd January*   St Genevieve

LOVE: A wonderfully sentimental and loving day.
LOOT: Splash out on love, laughter, leisure and pleasure.
LIFE: Make the most of your talents.
LUCK: ☋☋☋☋

A. M: *P. M:*

Born: John Thaw, 1942, actor
Event: Sir Edmund Hillary reaches South Pole, 1958

WEDNESDAY *4th January*   St Angela of Foligno

LOVE: Don't be impatient with loved ones or family.
LOOT: Quick thinking on your part could save you pounds.
LIFE: Put your mind to work.
LUCK: ☋

A. M: *P. M:*

Born: Dyan Cannon, 1939, US actress
Event: First appendicitis operation, 1885

THURSDAY 5th January
St Apollinaris

LOVE: Dealings with everyone you meet go well today.
LOOT: Don't get carried away on a spending spree!
LIFE: Thinking big about a working matter will bring rich rewards.
LUCK: ♡♡

A. M: P. M:

Born: Diane Keaton, 1946, US actress
Event: Catherine de' Medici, French Queen, died 1589

FRIDAY 6th January
St Erminold

LOVE: You'll hear from a loved one who lives far, far away.
LOOT: Buy something which provides food for thought.
LIFE: Cash in on any brainwaves - one could be a winner!
LUCK: ♡♡

A. M: P. M:

Born: Mel Gibson, 1959, US actor
Event: Harold crowned King of England, 1066

SATURDAY 7th January
St Lucian of Antioch

LOVE: A love affair is imbued with pungent passions.
LOOT: Beware of being too attached to your possessions now.
LIFE: Someone may try to use emotional blackmail on you.
LUCK: ♡♡♡

A. M: P. M:

Born: Helen Worth, 1951, TV actress
Event: Galileo discovers four satellites orbiting Jupiter, 1610

NOTES:

Sunday 1st January
New Moon in Capricorn

JANUARY						
S	M	T	W	T	F	S
1	2	3	4	5	6	7
8	9	10	11	12	13	14
15	16	17	18	19	20	21
22	23	24	25	26	27	28
29	30	31				

SUNDAY 8th January   St Severinus

LOVE: A relative could be spoiling for a fight.
LOOT: Going shopping? Then work out a budget and stick to it!
LIFE: Think about what you really want from your career.
LUCK: ʊʊ

A. M: *P. M:*

Born: David Bowie, 1947, Rock singer
Event: Rationing of butter, sugar and bacon in Britain, 1940

MONDAY 9th January   St Berhtwald of Canterbury

LOVE: Any partnership problems will come to a head today.
LOOT: Someone tries to twist you round their little finger.
LIFE: A career matter will make you see red.
LUCK: ʊʊ

A. M: *P. M:*

Born: Susannah York, 1942, actress
Event: Concorde first test flight, 1969

TUESDAY 10th January   St Agatho

LOVE: Clear the air with an amour, then forget all about it.
LOOT: Out on the town? Then let others have a say in what you're going to
         do.
LIFE: It's time to put your cards on the table workwise.
LUCK: ʊ

A. M: *P. M:*

Born: Rod Stewart, 1945, rock singer
Event: Penny Post begins in London, 1840

WEDNESDAY 11th January   St Salvius of Amiens

LOVE: Relationships couldn't be better, so enjoy them!
LOOT: A social event is enjoyable but expensive.
LIFE: Artistic ventures get a big boost today.
LUCK: ʊʊʊ

A. M: *P. M:*

Born: John Sessions, 1953, actor/comedian
Event: First women jurors sworn in at Old Bailey, 1921

THURSDAY 12th January — St Ailred

LOVE: Discuss your deepest feelings with a close chum.
LOOT: Don't commit yourself to anything pricey today.
LIFE: A workmate or client has an emotional effect on you.
LUCK: ☽☽☽☽

A. M: *P. M:*

Born: Michael Aspel, 1933, TV presenter
Event: Gregorian calendar introduced by Protestants in Switzerland, 1701

FRIDAY 13th January — St Hilary of Poitiers

LOVE: Bring out your sensitivity and sympathy.
LOOT: You may over-estimate the size of a domestic expense.
LIFE: You'll be bowled over by the kindness of a workmate.
LUCK: ☽

A. M: *P. M:*

Born: Stephen Hendry, 1969, snooker player
Event: 388-carat diamond mined at Kimberley, South Africa, 1919

SATURDAY 14th January — St Kentigern

LOVE: Get-togethers and gatherings will be great!
LOOT: If you're going shopping, treat yourself to a little luxury!
LIFE: You'll spend more time chatting than working now.
LUCK: ☽☽☽☽

A. M: *P. M:*

Born: Faye Dunaway, 1941, US actress
Event: Frost Fair held on Thames at London, 1814

NOTES:

Monday 16th January
Full Moon in Cancer

JANUARY						
S	M	T	W	T	F	S
1	2	3	4	5	6	7
8	9	10	11	12	13	14
15	16	17	18	19	20	21
22	23	24	25	26	27	28
29	30	31				

SUNDAY 15th January   St Paul of Thebes

LOVE: You'll enjoy being with sober and sensitive folk today.
LOOT: Weigh up the pros and cons before handing over cash.
LIFE: Discuss a working worry with a colleague.
LUCK: U

A. M: *P. M:*

Born: Martin Luther King, 1929, black civil rights leader
Event: Women accepted for degrees, first time at London University, 1878

MONDAY 16th January   St Honoratus

LOVE: A parent or older chum will be a tower of strength.
LOOT: Hard work may pay off in the shape of a promotion or bonus.
LIFE: Finish off any outstanding tasks today.
LUCK: U

A. M: *P. M:*

Born: Ethel Merman, 1909, US actress/singer
Event: Gulf War, Operation Desert Storm, began, 1991

TUESDAY 17th January   St Antony of Egypt

LOVE: Someone you meet every day will have a big effect on you.
LOOT: Need a new car? Then start thinking about it now.
LIFE: Advertise your talents in the coming months!
LUCK: UUUU

A. M: *P. M:*

Born: Muhammad Ali, 1942, boxer
Event: Captain Cook crossed the Antarctic Circle in the *Resolution*, 1773

WEDNESDAY 18th January   St Desle

LOVE: Enjoy the company of friends and your favourite folk.
LOOT: Buy something connected with a favourite hobby or pastime.
LIFE: A good day if you can bring out your artistic talents.
LUCK: U

A. M: *P. M:*

Born: Cary Grant, 1904, British film actor
Event: Captain Scott arrived at South Pole, 1912

THURSDAY 19th January St Wulfstan

LOVE: A romantic reverie could be ruined when one of you sees red.
LOOT: You won't stand for someone's underhand attitude to money.
LIFE: Pour oil on troubled waters if you get the chance.
LUCK: ∪

A. M: *P. M:*

Born: Stefan Edberg, 1966, tennis player
Event: Order of the Garter introduced by King Edward III, 1348

FRIDAY 20th January St Euthymius

LOVE: A love affair will be everything you wanted, and more.
LOOT: Treat yourself to a luxury or two!
LIFE: Capitalise on your creative capabilities!
LUCK: ∪∪∪∪

A. M: *P. M:*

Born: Liza Goddard, 1950, actress
Event: Mersey Tunnel opened by Prince of Wales, 1886

SATURDAY 21st January St Agnes

LOVE: Throw yourself into the social scene!
LOOT: You'll have a terrific time spending money on your favourite folk.
LIFE: Being honest with others will pay dividends now.
LUCK: ∪∪

A. M: *P. M:*

Born: Martin Shaw, 1945, actor
Event: Edward VIII proclaimed King, 1936

NOTES:

JANUARY

S	M	T	W	T	F	S
1	*2*	*3*	*4*	*5*	*6*	*7*
8	*9*	*10*	*11*	*12*	*13*	*14*
15	*16*	*17*	*18*	*19*	*20*	*21*
22	*23*	*24*	*25*	*26*	*27*	*28*
29	*30*	*31*				

SUNDAY 22nd January — St Timothy

LOVE: Friends will mean a lot to you in the coming months.
LOOT: The months ahead are a good time to join financial forces with friends.
LIFE: Future plans are about to take off in a big way.
LUCK: UUUU

A. M: *P. M:*

Born: John Hurt, 1940, actor
Event: Edward VII became King, 1901

MONDAY 23rd January — St Ildephonsus

LOVE: One of the family will do their best to upset the apple cart.
LOOT: A domestic expense may not be as serious as it seems.
LIFE: Keep your head down at work and keep out of conflicts.
LUCK: U

A. M: *P. M:*

Born: HRH Princess Caroline of Monaco, 1957
Event: House of Lords' proceedings televised for first time, 1985

TUESDAY 24th January — Saint Babylas

LOVE: Turn your fervent feelings into passion or amour.
LOOT: Don't blow your top if an outing costs more than you'd hoped.
LIFE: Work off your angst with an athletic or aesthetic activity.
LUCK: UU

A. M: *P. M:*

Born: Neil Diamond, 1941, singer/songwriter
Event: First Boy Scout troop formed, 1908

WEDNESDAY 25th January — St Apollo

LOVE: An amour may tell you a few home truths.
LOOT: Speak up if you feel hard-done-by moneywise.
LIFE: A good day to sort through papers or files.
LUCK: UU

A. M: *P. M:*

Born: Robert Burns, 1759, poet
Event: Henry VIII married Anne Boleyn, 1533

THURSDAY 26th January — St Paula

LOVE: A misunderstanding's likely in an *affaire de coeur*.
LOOT: Think twice before buying anything as you may not like it later.
LIFE: An artistic activity will be hit by a hiccup.
LUCK: ☾☾☾☾

A. M: P. M:

Born: Michael Bentine, 1922, comedian and writer
Event: Brazil discovered by Vicente Yanes Pinzon, 1500

FRIDAY 27th January — St Angela Merici

LOVE: You're attracting some very admiring glances!
LOOT: A shopping spree is fun but expensive!
LIFE: Communication is your key to success now.
LUCK: ☾☾

A. M: P. M:

Born: Wolfgang Amadeus Mozart, 1756, composer
Event: Thomas Edison patented the electric lamp, 1879

SATURDAY 28th January — St Thomas Aquinas

LOVE: Get to know a chum or a new neighbour.
LOOT: Shopping trips or jaunts to nearby towns will be grand.
LIFE: You won't let anyone make mincemeat of you today!
LUCK: ☾☾

A. M: P. M:

Born: Mikhail Baryshnikov, 1948, dancer
Event: King Henry VIII died, 1547

NOTES:

		JANUARY				
S	M	T	W	T	F	S
1	2	3	4	5	6	7
8	9	10	11	12	13	14
15	16	17	18	19	20	21
22	23	24	25	26	27	28
29	30	31				

SUNDAY 29th January   St Gildas

LOVE: A relative or poignant memory will prey on your mind.
LOOT: Buy something to beautify, enrich or enhance your home.
LIFE: It'll be difficult to keep your wits about you at work.
LUCK: U

A. M: *P. M:*

Born: John Junkin, 1930, actor/scriptwriter
Event: *Desert Island Discs* first broadcast, 1942

MONDAY 30th January   St Adelelmus

LOVE: An amour, pet or child will make life worth living.
LOOT: Why not treat yourself to a new outfit or wee trinket?
LIFE: Cash in on your creativity in career concerns!
LUCK: UUUU

A. M: *P. M:*

Born: Vanessa Redgrave, 1937, actress
Event: Sir Winston Churchill's State funeral, 1965

TUESDAY 31st January   St John Bosco

LOVE: Discuss your feelings with dear ones.
LOOT: Get more information if you're planning a major purchase.
LIFE: A simple conversation may solve a tricky problem.
LUCK: UU

A. M: *P. M:*

Born: Anna Pavlova, 1882, dancer
Event: Guy Fawkes executed, 1606

WEDNESDAY 1st February Ramadan Begins   St Bride

LOVE: You'll enjoy being with like-minded folk.
LOOT: Going out? Then take a friend or neighbour with you.
LIFE: Forge full steam ahead on ideas for your future success.
LUCK: UU

A. M: *P. M:*

Born: Muriel Spark, 1918, novelist
Event: End of clothes rationing in Britain, 1949

THURSDAY 2nd February — St Adalbald

LOVE: Try not to be at the beck and call of others.
LOOT: Why not buy something healthy but enjoyable?
LIFE: You'll feel put upon at work.
LUCK: ԾԾԾԾ

A. M: P. M:

Born: David Jason, 1940, actor
Event: Idi Amin declared himself absolute ruler of Uganda, 1971

FRIDAY 3rd February — St Anskar

LOVE:: Yakkety yak! Someone won't draw breath for a minute!
LOOT: Treat yourself to the theatre. cinema, or video at home.
LIFE: Tackle the things you really enjoy at work.
LUCK: ԾԾԾ

A. M: P. M:

Born: Val Doonican, 1929, singer
Event: The Soviet, Luna 9, reaches the moon and sends back TV pictures, 1966

SATURDAY 4th February — St Gilbert of Sempringham

LOVE: Family affairs take on a harmonious hue now.
LOOT: Invest money in your abode.
LIFE: Bring your creative and artistic talents to the fore.
LUCK: ԾԾԾԾ

A. M: P. M:

Born: Charles Augustus Lindbergh, 1902, US aviator
Event: Ceylon (Sri Lanka) gains Independence, 1948

NOTES:

Monday 30th January
New Moon in Aquarius
Start of the Chinese Year of the Pig

FEBRUARY						
S	M	T	W	T	F	S
			1	2	3	4
5	6	7	8	9	10	11
12	13	14	15	16	17	18
19	20	21	22	23	24	25
26	27	28				

SUNDAY 5th February — St Agatha

LOVE: Dealings with the clan leave a lot to be desired today.
LOOT: There may be a muddle over money matters.
LIFE: If you're at work you'd rather be at home.
LUCK: ☾

A. M: *P. M:*

Born: Russell Grant, 1952, astrologer
Event: The Prince of Wales declared Prince Regent, 1811

MONDAY 6th February — St Dorothy

LOVE: Enjoy the company of your favourite folk.
LOOT: Act the entrepreneur and prepare for success!
LIFE: A legal problem will start to sort itself out.
LUCK: ☾☾☾☾

A. M: *P. M:*

Born: Patrick MacNee, 1922, actor
Event: Succession of HM Queen Elizabeth II to the throne, 1952

TUESDAY 7th February — St Moses

LOVE: You're in the mood for love!
LOOT: A partner may take more than their fair share of your loot.
LIFE: Partners and associates are difficult to deal with.
LUCK: ☾☾

A. M: *P. M:*

Born: Dora Bryan, 1924, actress
Event: Most of the Dead Sea Scrolls found, 1947

WEDNESDAY 8th February — St Theodore

LOVE: Get involved in an altruistic or charitable activity.
LOOT: Someone close needs help on the financial front.
LIFE: You'll tune into an associate's mood in an instant.
LUCK: ☾

A. M: *P. M:*

Born: James Dean, 1931, US film actor
Event: Formation of the Confederate States of America, 1861

THURSDAY 9th February   St Teilo

LOVE: Why not visit someone whose company you really enjoy?
LOOT: Think about improving your current mode of transport.
LIFE: Be generous and big-hearted over professional affairs.
LUCK: ʊʊʊʊ

A. M: *P. M*:

Born: Sandy Lyle, 1958, golfer
Event: First performance of Verdi' *Falstaff*, 1893

FRIDAY 10th February   St Scholastica

LOVE: Social events or gatherings will be great.
LOOT: Why not buy yourself a treat or trinket?
LIFE: Work will take an enjoyable and productive turn.
LUCK: ʊʊʊ

A. M: *P. M*:

Born: Roberta Flack, 1938, US singer
Event: Queen Victoria married Prince Albert, 1840

SATURDAY 11th February   St Benedict of Aniane

LOVE: An older associate will come on strong.
LOOT: Stick to your budget for you're easily carried away today!
LIFE: You'll find any excuse to postpone projects.
LUCK: ʊ

A. M: *P. M*:

Born: Mary Quant, 1934, fashion designer
Event: Nelson Mandela released from prison after 27 years in South Africa, 1990

NOTES:

FEBRUARY						
S	M	T	W	T	F	S
			1	2	3	4
5	6	7	8	9	10	11
12	13	14	15	16	17	18
19	20	21	22	23	24	25
26	27	28				

SUNDAY 12th February   St Meletius

LOVE: Clear the air with a loved one, then forgive and forget.
LOOT: You'll discover the true cost of a recent social event.
LIFE: A plan for the future is about to sink or swim.
LUCK: ♋♋

A. M: P. M:

Born: Abraham Lincoln, 1809, 16th US President
Event: End of Manchu Dynasty, China became a Republic, 1912

MONDAY 13th February   St Agabus

LOVE: You're very sensitive now but are your impressions accurate?
LOOT: It's not a good day to make any major purchases.
LIFE: Folk in authority may make you feel inferior.
LUCK: ♋

A. M: P. M:

Born: Peter Gabriel, 1950, singer/songwriter
Event: Glencoe Massacre, the Campbells murdered the Macdonalds, 1692

TUESDAY 14th February   St Valentine

LOVE: Gregarious gatherings and social soirées are great.
LOOT: Talk to financial folk and ask for what you want.
LIFE: Good news about a plan that's very dear to your heart.
LUCK: ♋♋♋♋

A. M: P. M:

Born: Kevin Keegan, 1951, footballer
Event: St Valentine's Day Massacre, Chicago, 1929

WEDNESDAY 15th February   St Agape of Terni

LOVE: You're about to bid a friend a fond farewell.
LOOT: Sort out the funding for a future dream or scheme.
LIFE: If you're feeling the pinch then find ways round it.
LUCK: ♋♋♋

A. M: P. M:

Born: Claire Bloom, 1931, actress
Event: Britain changes to decimal currency, 1971

THURSDAY 16th February   St Falvian

LOVE: A loved one is in need of your help or support.
LOOT: If you're thinking of moving house then talk to experts.
LIFE: Look at all the details of a business plan.
LUCK: ☾☾☾☾

A. M: *P. M:*

Born: John McEnroe, 1959, US tennis player
Event: Fidel Castro became Cuban prime minister, 1959

FRIDAY 17th February   St Evermod

LOVE: Give and take in all close encounters today.
LOOT: A relative who needs help need look no further than you.
LIFE: You'll be moved by someone's plight or predicament.
LUCK: ☾

A. M: *P. M:*

Born: Julia Mckenzie, 1941, actress/singer
Event: Lord Carnavaron's team opened Tutankhamun's inner tomb at Luxor, 1923

SATURDAY 18th February   St Bernadette

LOVE: Seek out your favourite folk.
LOOT: Splash out on a wee treat or two.
LIFE: Put your feelings into precise and concise words.
LUCK: ☾☾☾☾

A. M: *P. M:*

Born: Ned Sherrin, 1931, TV and Radio presenter/producer
Event: Publication of John Bunyan's *Pilgrims Progress*, 1678

NOTES:

Wednesday 15th February
Full Moon in Leo

FEBRUARY

S	M	T	W	T	F	S
			1	2	3	4
5	6	7	8	9	10	11
12	13	14	15	16	17	18
19	20	21	22	23	24	25
26	27	28				

SUNDAY 19th February — St Barbatus

LOVE: Work will upset a social outing or plan.
LOOT: Don't expect to get something for nothing today.
LIFE: Stop letting a colleague or client take you for granted!
LUCK: ☻

A. M: P. M:

Born: HRH The Duke of York, 1960
Event: Thomas Edison patented the phonograph, 1878

MONDAY 20th February — St Wulfric

LOVE: A family matter needs to be sorted out though it'll be tricky at the time.
LOOT: Hassles over the housekeeping or home accounts rise to the surface.
LIFE: You're torn between duty and pleasure.
LUCK: ☻

A. M: P. M:
Born: Sidney Poitier, 1927, US film actor
Event: Assassination of James I of Scotland, 1437

TUESDAY 21st February — St Peter Damian

LOVE: Relax in the company of the ones you love best.
LOOT: Push the boat out if you've invited folk over to your place.
LIFE: You'll benefit from someone's protective attitude.
LUCK: ☻

A. M: P. M:

Born: Jilly Cooper, 1937, author/journalist
Event: Abolition of identity cards in Britain, 1952

WEDNESDAY 22nd February — St Baradates

LOVE: A heart-to-heart will be profound but open your eyes to the truth.
LOOT: Don't read more into a money worry than meets the eye.
LIFE: Discussions will go well only if you keep calm.
LUCK: ☻☻

A. M: P. M:

Born: Bruce Forsyth, 1928, entertainer
Event: Frank Winfield Woolworth's first store opened in New York, 1879

THURSDAY 23rd February   St Polycarp

LOVE: Spend time getting closer to someone you care about.
LOOT: A neighbour or community project needs your financial help.
LIFE: You'll hear good news about a workaday matter.
LUCK: ⋃⋃⋃⋃

A. M: *P. M:*

Born: Anton Mosimann, 1947, chef
Event: February Revolution began in Russia, 1917

FRIDAY 24th February   St Montanus

LOVE: Get out and about in convivial company.
LOOT: A letter or phone call brings good numismatic news.
LIFE: Workaday dealings are happy, harmonious and helpful.
LUCK: ⋃⋃

A. M: *P. M:*

Born: Denis Law, 1940, footballer
Event: 'Flying Scotsman' began service, 1923

SATURDAY 25th February   St Ethelbert

LOVE: Let love bring you closer to a special someone.
LOOT: You'll have second thoughts about a forthcoming treat.
LIFE: Make the most of your creative and organisational abilities.
LUCK: ⋃

A. M: *P. M:*

Born: George Harrison, 1943, former Beatle
Event: Abraham Lincoln's currency, 'greenbacks', was issued in USA, 1862

NOTES:

FEBRUARY						
S	M	T	W	T	F	S
			1	2	3	4
5	6	7	8	9	10	11
12	13	14	15	16	17	18
19	20	21	22	23	24	25
26	27	28				

SUNDAY 26th February   St Alexander

LOVE: Revel in the company of kith and kin or old chums.
LOOT: Find ways both big and small to beautify your abode.
LIFE: Don't expect too much from someone or you'll be disappointed.
LUCK: ʊʊ

A. M: P. M:

Born: Fats Domino, 1928, US singer
Event: First pound note issued by The Bank of England, 1797

MONDAY 27th February   St Leander

LOVE: Discuss your needs and desires with the one you love.
LOOT: Ask how much a treat or outing will cost.
LIFE: Keeping track of your thoughts will be difficult to say the least.
LOVE: ʊʊʊʊ

A. M: P. M:

Born: Elizabeth Taylor, 1932, actress
Event: Gulf War ends with liberation of Kuwait, 1991

TUESDAY 28th February (Shrove)   St Oswald of York

LOVE: Deal with the facts and abide by the truth.
LOOT: You'll have a nasty reminder about debts or IOUs.
LIFE: A workmate has a real power complex today.
LUCK: ʊʊ

A. M: P. M:

Born: Stephanie Beacham, 1949, actress
Event: Last British troops left India, 1948

WEDNESDAY 1st March (Ash)   St David

LOVE: A relative is acting out of character.
LOOT: Stand by for an unexpected household expense.
LIFE: A grand time to alter your employment prospects for the better.
LUCK: ʊʊʊ

A. M: P. M:

Born: Harry Belafonte, 1927, actor/singer
Event: The State of Pennsylvania abolished slavery in the US, 1780

THURSDAY 2nd March   St Chad

LOVE :   An aura of amour and affection envelops you this March.
LOOT: You'll be bowled over by a dear one's generosity.
LIFE: Cash in on your creativity in whichever way appeals.
LUCK: ℧℧℧℧

A. M: *P. M:*

Born: Mikhail Gorbachev, 1931, Russian Statesman
Event: Rhodesia created a Republic, 1970

FRIDAY 3rd March   St Ailred

LOVE: Discussions with dear ones will be very revealing indeed.
LOOT: A shopping trip has amazing consequences.
LIFE: A good day to convince someone of your skills and talents.
LUCK: ℧℧

A. M: *P. M:*

Born: Jean Harlow, 1911, US film actress
Event: The Star Spangled Banner was chosen as the U.S. national anthem, 1931

SATURDAY 4th March   St Casimir

LOVE: You think you know someone's motives, but what makes you so
         sure?
LOOT: An appliance or article is about to go on the blink or break down.
LIFE: Give a wide berth to tricksters, fraudsters or conmen.
LUCK: ℧℧℧℧

A. M: *P. M:*

Born: Patrick Moore, 1923, astronomer
Event: The first North Sea gas was piped ashore, 1967

NOTES:

Wednesday 1st March
New Moon in Pisces

MARCH						
S	M	T	W	T	F	S
			1	2	3	4
5	6	7	8	9	10	11
12	13	14	15	16	17	18
19	20	21	22	23	24	25
26	27	28	29	30	31	

SUNDAY *Lent 5th March*   St Adrian

LOVE: Take someone's words with a pinch or two of salt.
LOOT: Don't commit yourself to anything you can't deliver.
LIFE: Beware of taking on too much work now.
LUCK: ☋☋

A. M: *P. M:*

Born: Sir Rex Harrison, 1908, actor
Event: The Russian leader Joseph Stalin died, 1953

MONDAY *6th March*   St Chrodegang

LOVE: You're not in the mood to mix or mingle.
LOOT: Don't undersell yourself today.
LIFE: Your talents won't go unrecognised or unrewarded.
LUCK: ☋

A. M: *P. M:*

Born: Dame Kiri Te Kanawa, 1944, operatic soprano
Event: Ghana was granted Independence, 1957

TUESDAY *7th March*   St Perpetus

LOVE: Prepare for stormy seas with one particular partner.
LOOT: Postpone important cash concerns until you're more in the mood.
LIFE: Someone's trying to brainwash or browbeat you.
LUCK: ☋

A. M: *P. M:*

Born: Ivan Lendl, 1960, tennis player
Event:Transatlantic communication between New York and London
established, 1926

WEDNESDAY *8th March*   St Felix

LOVE: Let your affectionate and fond feelings flood out!
LOOT: Try to stick to your budget if you're off to the shops!
LIFE: The more artistic and creative you can be the better.
LUCK: ☋☋☋☋

A. M: *P. M:*

Born: Douglas Hurd, 1930, statesman
Event: Queen Anne was crowned, 1702

THURSDAY 9th March   St Frances of Rome

LOVE: A pal or partner will prove their worth today.
LOOT: Start planning a forthcoming outing or jaunt now.
LIFE: Talk to folk in the know about your future plans and ideas.
LUCK: ひひひひ

A. M: *P. M:*

Born: Vita Sackville-West, 1892, novelist
Event: Napoleon Bonaparte and Josephine de Beauharnais were married, 1796

FRIDAY 10th March   St John Ogilvie

LOVE: A dear one is difficult, dour or downhearted today.
LOOT: You've got to plough through reams of red tape.
LIFE: People in power are problematic now, but persevere.
LUCK: ひ

A. M: *P. M:*

Born: HRH Prince Edward, 1964
Event: The Bakerloo Line of London's underground was opened, 1906

SATURDAY 11th March   St Constantine

LOVE: A dear one is perturbed or pre-occupied today.
LOOT: You're in the right frame of mind to tackle major money matters.
LIFE: You'll gladly put your nose to the grindstone if needs be.
LUCK: ひ

A. M: *P. M:*

Born: Terence Alexander, 1923, actor
Event: Alexander Graham Bell made his first telephone communication, 1876

NOTES:

MARCH						
S	M	T	W	T	F	S
			1	2	3	4
5	6	7	8	9	10	11
12	13	14	15	16	17	18
19	20	21	22	23	24	25
26	27	28	29	30	31	

SUNDAY 12th March   St Gregory the Great

LOVE: Someone's running rings around you today.
LOOT: You get the wrong end of the stick about a family expense.
LIFE: Dealings with others are anything but easy now.
LUCK: ☋

A. M: P. M:

Born: Liza Minnelli, 1946, US actress/singer
Event: Mauritius granted Independence, 1968

MONDAY 13th March Commonwealth Day   St Nicephorus

LOVE: It's almost impossible to agree with pals and partners now.
LOOT: A future plan or ambition hits a financial hiccup today.
LIFE: You may have second thoughts about an associate.
LUCK: ☋

A. M: P. M:

Born: Neil Sedaka, 1939, singer/songwriter
Event: Sir William Herschel discovered the planet Uranus, 1781

TUESDAY 14th March   St Benedict

LOVE: You'll be torn between a pal and a partner.
LOOT: Keep finances and friends far apart today.
LIFE: Bring out your most creative side.
LUCK: ☋☋☋☋

A. M: P. M:

Born: Michael Caine, 1933, actor
Event: Karl Marx died, 1883

WEDNESDAY 15th March   St Clement Hofbauer

LOVE: A dear one acts in your own best interests now.
LOOT: A shopping trip is enjoyable but expensive.
LIFE: Cash in on your creativity.
LUCK: ☋☋☋☋

A. M: P. M:

Born: John Duttine, 1949, actor
Event: Abdication of Nicholas II, Tsar of Russia, 1917

THURSDAY 16th March   St Julian of Antioch

LOVE: Make an effort to help someone who can't help themselves.
LOOT: There may be a mix-up over a domestic bill.
LIFE: Try to understand a colleague's point of view.
LUCK: ☋☋☋

A. M: P. M:

Born: Leo McKern, 1920, actor
Event: Opening of the new London Bridge, 1973

FRIDAY 17th March   St Gertrude

LOVE: A chapter of rapture could come to an end now.
LOOT: Seek help if you can't carry your financial burden any longer.
LIFE: Your recent hard work is about to receive rich rewards!
LUCK: ☋

A. M: P. M:

Born: Nat 'King' Cole, 1919, US singer/pianist
Event: Oliver Cromwell abolishes the monarchy, England a commonwealth, 1649

SATURDAY 18th March   St Anselm of Lucca

LOVE: A delicious day when amour is all around you.
LOOT: Buy some super new spring clothes.
LIFE: The more creative your job the happier you are now.
LUCK: ☋☋☋

A. M: P. M:

Born: Pat Eddery, 1952, jockey
Event: US astronomer Clyde Tombaugh discovered the planet Pluto, 1930

NOTES:

Friday 17th March
Full Moon in Virgo

MARCH						
S	M	T	W	T	F	S
			1	2	3	4
5	6	7	8	9	10	11
12	13	14	15	16	17	18
19	20	21	22	23	24	25
26	27	28	29	30	31	

SUNDAY 19th March — St Joseph

LOVE: A day of difficult domestic disturbances and disruptions.
LOOT: One of the family seems to be spending your money for you.
LIFE: You've no truck with restrictions or routines today.
LUCK: ∪∪

A. M: P. M:

Born: Ursula Andress, 1936, US actress
Event: Official opening of Sydney Harbour bridge, 1932

MONDAY 20th March — St Cuthberts

LOVE: A relative will really make your day.
LOOT: Buy something to cheer up your abode.
LIFE: Be as original and innovative as possible.
LUCK: ∪∪

A. M: P. M:

Born: Dame Vera Lynn, 1917, singer
Event: King Henry IV died, 1413

TUESDAY 21st March — St Serapion of Thmuis

LOVE: A conversation or discussion comes as a revelation today.
LOOT: Thinking of buying a new car or bike? Then act now.
LIFE: A partner's opinions will take you by surprise.
LUCK: ∪∪∪∪

A. M: P. M:

Born: Ayrton Senna, 1960, Brazilian racing driver
Event: The new Waterloo Station in London was opened, 1922

WEDNESDAY 22nd March — St Catherine of Sweden

LOVE: Strengthen one particular partnership over the month ahead.
LOOT: Seek advice over important cash concerns.
LIFE: You'll fare best if you're part of a team now.
LUCK: ∪∪∪∪

A. M: P. M:

Born: William Shatner, 1931, US actor
Event: First international airline service, flying between Paris and Brussels, 1919

THURSDAY 23rd March St Turibius de Mongrovejo

LOVE: Surround yourself with convivial company today.
LOOT: A good day for shopping or buying presents.
LIFE: Pour oil on troubled working waters.
LUCK: ʊʊ

A. M: *P. M:*

Born: Barry Cryer, 1935, writer/comedian
Event: Adolf Hitler became German dictator, 1933

FRIDAY 24th March St Aldemar

LOVE: A new neighbour or colleague is great company now.
LOOT: Tie up contracts or sign on the dotted line today.
LIFE: Your optimistic attitude is extremely impressive!
LUCK: ʊʊʊ

A. M: *P. M:*

Born: Barbara Daly, 1945, make-up artist
Event: The English and Scottish crowns were united, 1603

SATURDAY 25th March St Alfwold

LOVE: A family member is vague, vacuous or vacillating.
LOOT: Doublecheck all household accounts.
LIFE: It's hard to concentrate on the task in hand today.
LUCK: ʊ

A. M: *P. M:*

Born: Elton John, 1947, singer/songwriter
Event: The modern Olympic Games first gold medal presented, 1896

NOTES:

MARCH						
S	M	T	W	T	F	S
			1	2	3	4
5	6	7	8	9	10	11
12	13	14	15	16	17	18
19	20	21	22	23	24	25
26	27	28	29	30	31	

SUNDAY 26th March Mid-Lent   St Basil the Younger

LOVE: Someone's being too critical or cutting for comfort.
LOOT: An expected pay-out or bonus doesn't arrive.
LIFE: Keep yourself to yourself in all career concerns now.
LUCK: ☽☽☽☽

A. M: *P. M:*

Born: Diana Ross, 1944, US singer
Event:The first driving tests introduced in Britain, 1934

MONDAY 27th March   St Alkeld

LOVE: Someone you meet through work means a lot to you now.
LOOT: A good time to plead your cash case or ask for a rise at work.
LIFE: Give a colleague the benefit of the doubt.
LUCK: ☽

A. M: *P. M:*

Born: Michael York, 1942, actor
Event: Formation of the US Navy, 1794

TUESDAY 28th March   St Guntramnus

LOVE: You're upset or unsettled when someone comes on too strong.
LOOT: Don't let a money worry turn into a drama.
LIFE: Clear the air with colleagues, clients or customers.
LUCK: ☽

A. M: *P. M:*

Born: Dirk Bogarde, 1921, actor/author
Event: Electric lighting installed in the Houses of Parliament, 1878

WEDNESDAY 29th March   St Armogastes

LOVE: Someone's feeling embarrassed or guilty about you.
LOOT: Don't be surprised if folk expect something for nothing now.
LIFE: A day when hard graft brings little reward.
LUCK: ☽☽☽

A. M: *P. M:*

Born: John Major MP, 1943
Event: The Royal Albert Hall was opened by Queen Victoria, 1871

THURSDAY 30th March   St John Climacus

LOVE: Seek out folk who are less fortunate than yourself.
LOOT: Try to boost someone's coffers.
LIFE: A good day for listening to others.
LUCK: ☋

A. M: *P. M:*

Born: Eric Clapton, 1945, guitarist/songwriter
Event: The Treaty of Paris was signed to end the Crimean war, 1856

FRIDAY 31st March   St Acacius

LOVE: Why not woo your other half all over again?
LOOT: Seek the advice of folk in the financial know now.
LIFE: Partnerships are starred for success in the days ahead.
LUCK: ☋☋☋☋

A. M: *P. M:*

Born: Sir David Steel, 1939, politician
Event: The first monthly installment of Charles Dickens', *Pickwick Papers*, 1836

SATURDAY 1st April   St Hugh of Grenoble

LOVE: A love affair or VIP of your heart is about to appear out of thin air!
LOOT: Why not turn a spare time concern into a little pin money?
LIFE: Keep track of important paperwork and documents now.
LUCK: ☋☋☋

A. M: *P. M:*

Born: George Baker, 1931, actor/writer
Event: Warsaw Pact's military element disbanded, 1991

NOTES:

Friday 31st March
New Moon in Aries

APRIL						
S	M	T	W	T	F	S
						1
2	3	4	5	6	7	8
9	10	11	12	13	14	15
16	17	18	19	20	21	22
23	24	25	26	27	28	29
30						

SUNDAY 2nd April   St Francis of Paola

LOVE: Cash in on your gift for compromise over the fortnight ahead.
LOOT: Get to the bottom of a money mystery.
LIFE: Your powers of concentration are ace now.
LUCK: ☽☽☽

A. M: *P. M:*

Born: Linford Christie, 1960, athlete
Event: The first broadcast of the Oxford and Cambridge Boat Race, 1927

MONDAY 3rd April   St Richard of Chichester

LOVE: A delicious day for caring and sharing.
LOOT: You'll benefit from someone's generosity.
LIFE: Make an effort to get closer to an associate.
LUCK: ☽

A. M: *P. M:*

Born: Doris Day, 1924, US actress/singer
Event: Haile Selassie proclaimed Emperor of Ethiopia, 1930

TUESDAY 4th April   St Isidore of Seville

LOVE: Let a loved one down gently today.
LOOT: Think about how to make a dream come true.
LIFE: Forge full steam ahead in a pet project.
LUCK: ☽

A. M: *P. M:*

Born: Muddy Waters, 1915, US blues singer/songwriter
Event: Francis Drake was knighted by Queen Elizabeth I, 1581

WEDNESDAY 5th April   St Juliana of Liege

LOVE: Grab the opportunity to get to know someone better.
LOOT: A good day to make a major purchase.
LIFE: Negotiations and discussions go like clockwork.
LUCK: ☽☽☽☽

A. M: *P. M:*

Born: Bette Davis, 1908, US film actress
Event: First automatic driverless trains operated on London's rail network, 1964

THURSDAY 6th April   St Celestine

LOVE: Don't read more into someone's flirting than meets the eye.
LOOT: Double-check tickets, timetables and itineraries today.
LIFE: Someone has a good idea, but will it work?
LUCK: ՍՍ

A. M: *P. M:*

Born: Harry Houdini, 1874, US escapologist
Event: St Paul's Cathedral damaged by earth tremor, 1580

FRIDAY 7th April   St Hegesippus

LOVE: Show a special someone that they're not forgotten.
LOOT: Why not splash out a little hard-earned cash?
LIFE: A colleague or boss is appreciative and approachable.
LUCK: ՍՍ

A. M: *P. M:*

Born: Billie Holiday, 1915, US singer
Event: The metre declared the official measurement of length in France, 1795

SATURDAY 8th April   St Agabus

LOVE: You'll have to walk on egg shells around one particular person.
LOOT: Red tape or needless bureaucracy gets you fighting mad.
LIFE: Don't upset a boss or superior just for the sake of it.
LUCK: ՍՍ

A. M: *P. M:*

Born: Dorothy Tutin, 1931, actress
Event: Juan Ponce de Leon discovered Florida, 1513

NOTES:

APRIL						
S	M	T	W	T	F	S
						1
2	3	4	5	6	7	8
9	10	11	12	13	14	15
16	17	18	19	20	21	22
23	24	25	26	27	28	29
30						

SUNDAY 9th April Palm Sunday   St Gaucherius

LOVE: Surround yourself with the folk you love best.
LOOT: Boodle's burning a hole in your pocket.
LIFE: You'll meet just the right person careerwise.
LUCK: ʊʊʊ

A. M: *P. M:*

Born: Hannah Gordon, 1941, actress
Event: Captain Cook discovered Botany Bay, Australia, 1770

MONDAY 10th April   St Fulbert

LOVE: The love of your life is about to take you by surprise.
LOOT: Try to spot the potential in a creative hobby or scheme.
LIFE: Your sense of status and satisfaction is on the up and up.
LUCK: ʊʊʊʊ

A. M: *P. M:*

Born: Omar Sharif, 1932, actor
Event: The first bananas on sale in London, 1633

TUESDAY 11th April   St Gemma Galgani

LOVE: Examine your motives over a dear one.
LOOT: Be honest if you've made slip-ups with some cash.
LIFE: Try to ignore someone's heavy-handed tactics.
LUCK: ʊ

A. M: *P. M:*

Born: Jill Gascoine, 1938, actress
Event: Napoleon banished to the Isle of Elba, 1814

WEDNESDAY 12th April   St Julius

LOVE: You'll enjoy an outing or jaunt with a pal or partner.
LOOT: Buy something associated with a hobby or pursuit.
LIFE: A great day to plan for the future.
LUCK: ʊʊʊʊ

A. M: *P. M:*

Born: Alan Ayckbourn, 1939, playwright
Event: Yuri Gagarin made the first manned space flight, 1961

THURSDAY *13th April Maundy Thursday*   St Martin

LOVE: A budding relationship has a touch of frostbite.
LOOT: The cash you counted on may not arrive after all.
LIFE: A colleague gives you the cold shoulder today.
LUCK: ☾

A. M: *P. M:*

Born: Gary Kasparov, 1963, Chess champion
Event: The first performance of Handel's *The Messiah*, 1742

FRIDAY *14th April Good Friday*   St Antony

LOVE: Expect the unexpected with partners today.
LOOT: Someone's attitude to cash is completely contrary.
LIFE: You've no patience now for folk who want to toe the line.
LUCK: ☾☾☾☾

A. M: *P. M:*

Born: Julie Christie, 1940, actress
Event: Abraham Lincoln was assassinated by John Wilkes Booth, 1865

SATURDAY *15th April*   St Aristarchus

LOVE: The time has come to tell a partner exactly what you think - and
         why.
LOOT: Been living beyond your means? Then tighten your belt now.
LIFE: Folk need to know where you stand, so don't prevaricate.
LUCK: ☾☾

A. M: *P. M:*

Born: Emma Thompson, 1959, actress
Event:The first five-pound note issued by The Bank of England, 1793

NOTES:

Saturday 15th April
Full Moon in Libra

APRIL						
S	M	T	W	T	F	S
						1
2	3	4	5	6	7	8
9	10	11	12	13	14	15
16	17	18	19	20	21	22
23	24	25	26	27	28	29
30						

SUNDAY 16th April Easter Day   St Bernadette

LOVE: What a fuss someone's making! Is it you?
LOOT: A friend gets heated and het up over a financial affair.
LIFE: It's not a good day to ask for favours or help.
LUCK: U

A. M: P. M:

Born: Gabriella Sabatini, 1970, tennis player
Event: Charles Edward Stuart, the Young Pretender, defeated at Culloden, 1746

MONDAY 17th April   St Agapetus

LOVE: Your amour makes a startling suggestion!
LOOT: Try not to buy anything on the spur of the moment.
LIFE: Folk react in unpredictable ways today.
LUCK: UU

A. M: P. M:

Born: Clare Francis, 1946, novelist/yachtswoman
Event: Introduction of Premium Savings Bonds in Britain, 1956

TUESDAY 18th April   St Apollonius the Apologist

LOVE: Make amends if you've fallen out with a relative.
LOOT: A great day to beautify your abode.
LIFE: Conciliation and consideration characterise all career concerns.
LUCK: UUUU

A. M: P. M:

Born: Hayley Mills, 1946, actress
Event: San Francisco devastated by a major earthquake, 1906

WEDNESDAY 19th April   St Alphege

LOVE: Visit a neighbour or get to know someone you see every day.
LOOT: Household bills or shopping trips could be costly today.
LIFE: Forge a new understanding with a workmate.
LUCK: UU

A. M: P. M:

Born: Dudley Moore, 1935, actor/musician
Event: Lord Byron died, 1824

THURSDAY 20th April — St Agnes of Montepulciano

LOVE: Intimate affairs are about to get a great big boost!
LOOT: Expect the unexpected in all official money matters today.
LIFE: You'll have to cope with someone's inflated ego.
LUCK: ☾☾

A. M: P. M:

Born: Nicholas Lyndhurst, 1961, actor
Event: Captain Cook discovered New South Wales, Australia, 1770

FRIDAY 21st April — St Anastasius

LOVE: Someone's about to show their jealous or possessive side.
LOOT: Your spiritual and material priorities are about to be changed forever.
LIFE: The lessons you learn now will be hard but worthwhile.
LUCK: ☾

A. M: P. M:

Born: HM the Queen, 1926
Event: Rome was founded, 753BC

SATURDAY 22nd April — St Alexander

LOVE: Fallen out with a partner? Then start building bridges now.
LOOT: Someone's got some important financial advice.
LIFE: Teamwork is your best bet over the coming month.
LUCK: ☾☾☾

A. M: P. M:

Born: Lloyd Honeyghan, 1960, welterweight boxing champion
Event: The first South Australia parliament opened, 1857

NOTES:

	APRIL					
S	M	T	W	T	F	S
						1
2	3	4	5	6	7	8
9	10	11	12	13	14	15
16	17	18	19	20	21	22
23	24	25	26	27	28	29
30						

SUNDAY 23rd April   St George

LOVE: Seek out your favourite folk and enjoy yourself.
LOOT: You're touched by someone's generosity.
LIFE: It's a great day to enlist the support of others.
LUCK: ○○○○

A. M: *P. M:*

Born: Shirley Temple, 1928, former child actress
Event: Decimal coins were issued in Britain, 1968

MONDAY 24th April   St Egbert

LOVE: Iron out any problems with a partner.
LOOT: A good day to concentrate on investments and official money
        matters.
LIFE: Workmates are helpful and friendly.
LUCK: ○○

A. M: *P. M:*

Born: Shirley Maclaine, 1934, US film actress/writer
Event: Gambia proclaimed a Republic, 1970

TUESDAY 25th April   St Mark

LOVE: Want to bowl someone over? Then have a go today!
LOOT: State your case and put your ideas forward to financial folk.
LIFE: Not a day to hide your light under a bushel.
LUCK: ○○○

A. M: *P. M:*

Born: Ella Fitzgerald, 1918, US singer
Event: The guillotine erected in Paris, 1792

WEDNESDAY 26th April   St Franca of Piacenza

LOVE: Whatever you say is wrong as far as one person is concerned.
LOOT: Someone helps themselves to what's rightfully yours.
LIFE: Try not to take every comment as outright criticism.
LUCK: ○

A. M: *P. M:*

Born: David Coleman, 1926, sports commentator
Event: Unification of Tanganyika and Zanzibar to form Tanzania, 1964

THURSDAY 27th April   St Zita

LOVE: A family matter will worry you over the months ahead.
LOOT: Go through joint accounts and official money matters today.
LIFE: Concentrate on details rather than big plans now.
LUCK: ✆✆✆✆

A. M: P. M:

Born: Sheena Easton, 1959, singer/actress
Event: Opening of the London Zoological Gardens, Regent's Park, 1828

FRIDAY 28th April   St Peter Chanel

LOVE: You're only hearing half the story from a loved one.
LOOT: Be careful about who you trust with your cash today.
LIFE: A partner is saying one thing and doing another.
LUCK: ✆✆

A. M: P. M:

Born: Ann-Margret, 1941, Swedish actress
Event: Fletcher Christian led the mutiny aboard HMS Bounty, 1789

SATURDAY 29th April   St Catherine of Siena

LOVE: Someone's about to have a mesmeric or intense effect on you.
LOOT: It's the perfect time to invest in providing for your future.
LIFE: Join forces with others for the best results now.
LUCK: ✆

A. M: P. M:

Born: Duke Ellington, 1899, US jazz composer/band leader
Event: The first performance in London of the musical, *Oklahoma!*, 1947

NOTES:

Saturday 29th April
Eclipsed New Moon in Taurus

APRIL						
S	M	T	W	T	F	S
						1
2	3	4	5	6	7	8
9	10	11	12	13	14	15
16	17	18	19	20	21	22
23	24	25	26	27	28	29
30						

SUNDAY 30th April — St James the Great

LOVE: You'll be happiest in the company of dear ones.
LOOT: A relative or associate needs a little loot.
LIFE: A chat or conversation sparks off a brilliant brainwave.
LUCK: ∪

A. M: *P. M:*

Born: Leslie Grantham, 1946, actor
Event: Inauguration of the 1st American president, General George Washington, 1789

MONDAY 1st May — St Asaph

LOVE: A partner or relative takes their mood out on you.
LOOT: Check the balance on a joint account before dipping into it.
LIFE: Someone thinks they're being a help, but are they really?
LUCK: ∪∪

A. M: *P. M:*

Born: Joanna Lumley, 1946, actress
Event: The Empire State Building was opened in New York, 1931

TUESDAY 2nd May — St Athanasius

LOVE: You're only interested in folk who are a wee bit different today.
LOOT: Sign up for a trip or jaunt that's exciting and adventurous.
LIFE: Approach an old problem from a new angle.
LUCK: ∪∪∪

A. M: *P. M:*

Born: Jimmy White, 1962, snooker player
Event: Leonardo da Vinci died, 1519

WEDNESDAY 3rd May — St Phillip & St James

LOVE: It's not a day to go it alone, for the social scene looks smashing!
LOOT: A good opportunity to make major purchases for you or another.
LIFE: Don't start any big projects unless you know you'll finish them!
LUCK: ∪∪∪∪

A. M: *P. M:*

Born: Henry Cooper, 1934, heavyweight boxing champion
Event: Columbus discovered Jamaica, 1494

THURSDAY 4th May   St Gotthard

LOVE: Bury the hatchet with your other half or an older pal.
LOOT: Go through joint accounts or big business arrangements.
LIFE: You'll do best as part of a team today.
LUCK: ☋

A. M: *P. M:*

Born: Audrey Hepburn, 1929, film actress/UNICEF ambassador
Event: Diomed won the first Derby to be run at Epsom, 1780

FRIDAY 5th May   St Hilary of Arles

LOVE: Anything goes in amorous affairs all summer long!
LOOT: Luxuries and treats may not live up to expectations.
LIFE: A project close to your heart is about to hit hiccups and hitches.
LUCK: ☋☋

A. M: *P. M:*

Born: Michael Palin, 1943, actor/comedian
Event: Napoleon Bonaparte, Emperor of France died, 1821

SATURDAY 6th May   St Edbert

LOVE: A friend is exhilarating, inspiring and unforgettable.
LOOT: You want to buy something unusual but will you still like it
      tomorrow?
LIFE: A creative or artistic project doesn't go according to plan.
LUCK: ☋☋

A. M: *P. M:*

Born: Orson Welles, 1915, US actor/director/writer
Event: The Penny Black postage stamp was issued, 1840

NOTES:

			MAY			
S	M	T	W	T	F	S
	1	2	3	4	5	6
7	8	9	10	11	12	13
14	15	16	17	18	19	20
21	22	23	24	25	26	27
28	29	30	31			

SUNDAY 7th May   St John of Beverly

LOVE: Someone's suffering from the green-eyed monster.
LOOT: A joint account or kitty is in the red but who's to blame?
LIFE: Folk aren't nearly as co-operative as you'd like.
LUCK: ☂☂☂☂

A. M: *P. M:*

Born: Richard O'Sullivan, 1944, actor
Event: Nelson's flagship, HMS Victory, was launched at Chatham, 1765

MONDAY 8th May   St John

LOVE: Seek out the company of convivial and congenial chums.
LOOT: Enrol in a group or gathering of like-minded folk.
LIFE: A good day to win friends and influence people!
LUCK: ☂

A. M: *P. M:*

Born: Gary Glitter, 1944, rock singer
Event: Restoration of the monarchy, 1660

TUESDAY 9th May   St Beatus of Lungern

LOVE: You aren't acting as rationally and objectively as you imagine.
LOOT: Someone's spendthrift or impecunious ways call for action.
LIFE: A colleague says one thing then does another.
LUCK: ☂☂☂

A. M: *P. M:*

Born: Joan Sims, 1930, actress
Event: The first electric lights in Piccadilly Circus, 1932

WEDNESDAY 10th May   St Antoninus

LOVE: Reach a new understanding with someone very special.
LOOT: You'll realise today exactly where your pecuniary priorities lie.
LIFE: A problem or hitch sorts itself out all by itself today.
LUCK: ☂

A. M: *P. M:*

Born: Fred Astaire, 1899, US dancer/actor
Event: During air raids on London, the House of Commons was destroyed, 1941

THURSDAY 11th May   St Cyril

LOVE: Seek out folk who are alive, vibrant and exciting.
LUCK: Be daring! Buy something a wee bit different!
LIFE: Make the most of your creative capabilities.
LUCK: ʊʊ

A. M: P. M:

Born: Dame Margaret Rutherford, 1892, actress
Event: Constantinople became the new capital of the Roman Empire, AD 330

FRIDAY 12th May   St Epiphanius

LOVE: Not a day to go it alone for you need plenty of lively company now.
LUCK: Consult interested parties before making any financial decisions.
LIFE: Push a new plan forward with the help of others.
LUCK: ʊʊʊ

A. M: P. M:

Born: Susan Hampshire, 1942, actress
Event: The coronation of King George VI and Queen Elizabeth, 1937

SATURDAY 13th May   St Andrew Hubert Fournet

LOVE: One of the clan expects some very saintly behaviour from you, but will they get it?
LUCK: A household expense needs watching as it could get out of hand.
LIFE: Is someone trying to undermine your confidence?
LUCK: ʊ

A. M: P. M:

Born: Selina Scott, 1951, TV presenter
Event: The first English settlement was made at Jamestown, Virginia, 1607

NOTES:

			MAY			
S	M	T	W	T	F	S
	1	2	3	4	5	6
7	8	9	10	11	12	13
14	15	16	17	18	19	20
21	22	23	24	25	26	27
28	29	30	31			

SUNDAY 14th May   St Matthais

LOVE: Scotch even a hint of jealousy or envy before it gets a hold.
LOOT: You need to revise, review and reconstruct your fiscal policy.
LIFE: Your work priorities are changing, but has your job altered accordingly?
LUCK: ☋

A. M: *P. M:*

Born: Francesca Annis, 1945, actress
Event: Louis XIV became King of France, aged four, 1643

MONDAY 15th May   St Rupert

LOVE: A loved one's unpredictable ways affect you for good or ill.
LOOT: Don't buy things on the spur of the moment or you'll regret it.
LIFE: An outrageous idea could be worth its weight in gold.
LUCK: ☋☋

A. M: *P. M:*

Born: James Mason, 1909, actor
Event: The Theatre Royal Covent Garden was opened, 1858

TUESDAY 16th May Middlesex Day   St Brendan

LOVE: A relationship is about to take a very serious and emotional turn.
LOOT: Buy a treat or two for a very special someone.
LIFE: Think about joining forces with like-minded folk.
LUCK: ☋☋☋☋

A. M: *P. M:*

Born: Roy Hudd, 1936, comedian
Event: The first Academy Awards were held in Hollywood, 1929

WEDNESDAY 17th May   St Robert Bellarmine

LOVE: What's got into your other half? You can't do anything right.
LOOT: It's not a good day to commit yourself to anything expensive or binding.
LIFE: You do something that seems like a good idea, though later you're not so sure.
LUCK: ☋☋

A. M: *P. M:*
Born: Dennis Potter, 1935, playwright
Event: Queen Victoria laid the foundation stone of the Victoria & Albert Museum, 1899

THURSDAY 18th May   St John I

LOVE: A loved one is determined to extract their pound of flesh from you.
LOOT: Someone over-reacts about cash concerns.
LIFE: A skirmish with a partner or associate looks more than likely.
LUCK: ☋☋☋

A. M: P. M:

Born: His Holiness the Pope, John Paul II, 1920
Event: Napoleon proclaimed Emperor of France, 1804

FRIDAY 19th May   St Dunstan

LOVE: Show a partner or associate how generous you can be.
LOOT: Discuss pecuniary plans with interested parties.
LIFE: Work in harmony with others whenever you get the chance.
LUCK: ☋☋

A. M: P. M:

Born: James Fox, 1939, actor
Event: The Spanish Armada sailed from Lisbon, 1588

SATURDAY 20th May   St Bernardino of Siena

LOVE: A dear one pushes you too far and has to deal with the
         consequences.
LOOT: Try not to be heavy-handed in any material matters.
LIFE: You'll reach stalemate fast if you cross swords with associates
         today.
LUCK: ☋☋☋☋

A. M: P. M:
Born: James Stewart, 1908, US film actor
Event: Charles Lindbergh first non-stop transatlantic solo flight to Paris, 1927

NOTES:

Sunday 14th May
Full Moon in Scorpio

			MAY			
S	M	T	W	T	F	S
	1	2	3	4	5	6
7	8	9	10	11	12	13
14	15	16	17	18	19	20
21	22	23	24	25	26	27
28	29	30	31			

SUNDAY 21st May   St Helena

LOVE: A day for seeking out exciting and invigorating companions.
LOOT: Booking a trip or holiday? Then choose a venue you've never
          visited before.
LIFE: Increase your understanding of the world and its ways today.
LUCK: ∪∪

A. M: *P. M:*

Born: Harold Robbins, 1916, US novelist
Event: Summer Time began in Britain, 1916

MONDAY 22nd May   St Rita of Casica

LOVE: A pal or partner isn't as sympathetic or understanding as you'd
          hoped.
LOOT: Not a good day to ask for loans, mortgages or other financial help.
LIFE: You'll feel like a slave or skivvy today but don't act the martyr.
LUCK: ∪

A. M: *P. M:*

Born: Laurence Olivier, 1907, actor
Event: Ceylon became a Republic with the new name, Sri Lanka, 1972

TUESDAY 23rd May   St Ivo of Chartres

LOVE: A friend acts more like a foe today.
LOOT: Skirmishes and clashes look likely, especially where your social life
          is concerned.
LIFE: A plan or hope for the future blows a big fuse.
LUCK: ∪

A. M: *P. M:*

Born: Joan Collins, 1933, actress
Event: Joan of Arc taken prisoner by the English, 1430

WEDNESDAY 24th May   St Vincent of Lerins

LOVE: It'll seem that someone's trying to take advantage of you between
          now and mid-June.
LOOT: Double-check tickets, timetables and passports if you're about to go
          away.
LIFE: Something that seemed a certainty will soon look less likely to
          happen.
LUCK: ∪∪∪∪

A. M: *P. M:*
Born: Bob Dylan, 1941, US singer
Event: Westminster bridge was opened in London, 1862

THURSDAY 25th May St Aldhelm

LOVE: Sex and desire are about to take a back seat or become hush-hush.
LOOT: A charitable or philanthropic cause will appeal to you, body and soul.
LIFE: Try to spend the next two months working by yourself or behind the scenes.
LUCK: ᑌ

A. M: *P. M:*

Born: Ian McKellen, 1939, actor
Event: Jesse Owens broke five world records at the Olympic Games in Berlin, 1936

FRIDAY 26th May St Philip Neri

LOVE: There's no knowing what a loved one will do or say today.
LOOT: Try to curb impulsive spending for you may not like things once you've bought them.
LIFE: You've no time for partners urging caution or care now.
LUCK: ᑌᑌ

A. M: *P. M:*

Born: Peter Cushing, 1913, actor
Event: Mount Etna in Sicily began a series of devastating eruptions, 1870

SATURDAY 27th May St Augustine of Canterbury

LOVE: You're bowled over by a surge of deep emotion for that special someone.
LOOT: Dip into the joint account to buy a treat for you and your other half.
LIFE: Associates and partners are easily won over to your side today.
LUCK: ᑌ

A. M: *P. M:*

Born: Cilla Black, 1943, singer/entertainer
Event: Peter the Great founded St Petersburg, 1703

NOTES:

MAY

S	M	T	W	T	F	S
	1	*2*	*3*	*4*	*5*	*6*
7	*8*	*9*	*10*	*11*	*12*	*13*
14	*15*	*16*	*17*	*18*	*19*	*20*
21	*22*	*23*	*24*	*25*	*26*	*27*
28	*29*	*30*	*31*			

SUNDAY 28th May *Sunday after Ascension* St Germanus of Paris

LOVE: There's a surprise concerning a loved one but it'll all work out for the best.
LOOT: You've got itchy feet today so invest in an enjoyable trip or jaunt.
LIFE: Approach a project from a new angle and see the difference it makes.
LUCK: ᘉᘉ

A. M: *P. M:*
Born: Thora Hird, 1916, actress
Event: The first London production of the musical, *Guys and Dolls*, 1953

MONDAY 29th May *Bank Holiday*   St Bernard of Montjoux

LOVE: The wisdom, knowledge and optimism of a certain someone makes a big impact now.
LOOT: You're in the mood to go travelling, so browse through brochures.
LIFE: Opportunity is knocking, so let it in quick!
LUCK: ᘉᘉᘉ

A. M: *P. M:*

Born: Nanette Newman, 1939, actress/writer
Event: Sir Edmund Hillary & Sherpa Tenzing reached peak of Mount Everest, 1953

TUESDAY 30th May   St Joan of Arc

LOVE: You feel withdrawn and distant from the folk you meet today.
LOOT: You're prone to impulsive spending sprees now.
LIFE: Something you thought was a good idea gets a big thumbs down.
LUCK: ᘉ

A. M: *P. M:*

Born: Bob Willis, 1949, cricketer
Event: Joan of Arc was burnt at the stake at Rouen, 1431

WEDNESDAY 31st May *Muslim New Year (1416)*   St Cantius

LOVE: It's a perfect day for talking seriously to a parent or older pal.
LOOT: Find ways of making your money work harder for you.
LIFE: You'll do well now whether behind the scenes or in the spotlight.
LUCK: ᘉ

A. M: *P. M:*

Born: Terry Waite, 1939, Anglican emissary
Event: The Union of South Africa became a Republic, 1961

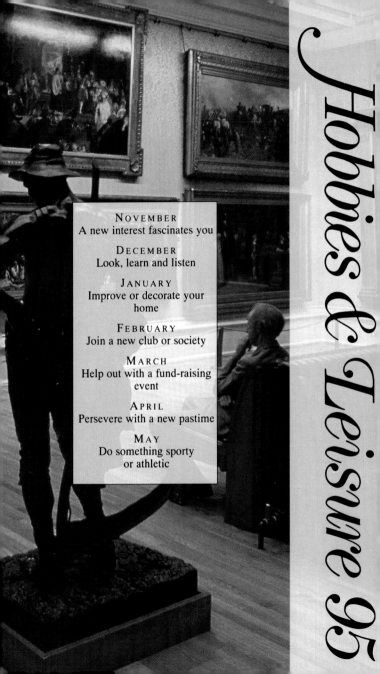

NOVEMBER
A new interest fascinates you

DECEMBER
Look, learn and listen

JANUARY
Improve or decorate your
home

FEBRUARY
Join a new club or society

MARCH
Help out with a fund-raising
event

APRIL
Persevere with a new pastime

MAY
Do something sporty
or athletic

Hobbies & Leisure 95

Travel 95

NOVEMBER
Visit nearby folk

DECEMBER
Get away for Christmas

JANUARY
Seek expert advice if unsure
where to go

FEBRUARY
A friend invites you to stay
with them

MARCH
Go away with a close partner

APRIL
Have a romantic trip with the
one you love

MAY
A grand month to go
travelling

JUNE
Short trips are fascinating

JULY
Visit kith and kin

AUGUST
Head for familiar places

SEPTEMBER
Beware of a gyppy tummy

OCTOBER
Journeys near and far
are fun

NOVEMBER
Start saving seriously for
a trip

DECEMBER
Travel in your mind

Fashion 95

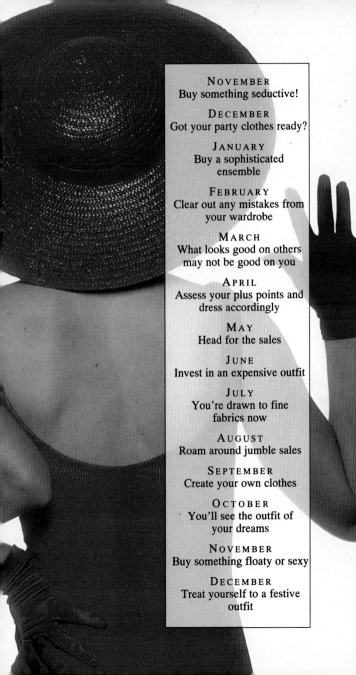

NOVEMBER
Buy something seductive!

DECEMBER
Got your party clothes ready?

JANUARY
Buy a sophisticated
ensemble

FEBRUARY
Clear out any mistakes from
your wardrobe

MARCH
What looks good on others
may not be good on you

APRIL
Assess your plus points and
dress accordingly

MAY
Head for the sales

JUNE
Invest in an expensive outfit

JULY
You're drawn to fine
fabrics now

AUGUST
Roam around jumble sales

SEPTEMBER
Create your own clothes

OCTOBER
You'll see the outfit of
your dreams

NOVEMBER
Buy something floaty or sexy

DECEMBER
Treat yourself to a festive
outfit

Gardening 95

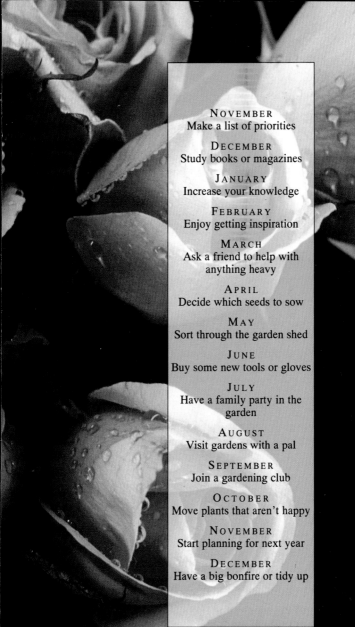

NOVEMBER
Make a list of priorities

DECEMBER
Study books or magazines

JANUARY
Increase your knowledge

FEBRUARY
Enjoy getting inspiration

MARCH
Ask a friend to help with
anything heavy

APRIL
Decide which seeds to sow

MAY
Sort through the garden shed

JUNE
Buy some new tools or gloves

JULY
Have a family party in the
garden

AUGUST
Visit gardens with a pal

SEPTEMBER
Join a gardening club

OCTOBER
Move plants that aren't happy

NOVEMBER
Start planning for next year

DECEMBER
Have a big bonfire or tidy up

Hobbies & Leisure 95

JUNE
Go for long walks or hikes

JULY
You'll be intrigued by a new hobby

AUGUST
Spend time with friends

SEPTEMBER
You're busy but make time for yourself

OCTOBER
Give your home a facelift

NOVEMBER
Visit art galleries or other cultural venues

DECEMBER
Throw open the doors of your abode!

THURSDAY 1st June — St Justin Martyr

LOVE: A chat or conversation will be illuminating, informative and fascinating.
LOOT: Voyages, journeys and jaunts are tempting you to go travelling.
LIFE: Don't let the grass grow under your feet - make the most of today's opportunities.
LUCK: ʊʊʊʊ

A. M: *P. M:*
Born: Robert Powell, 1944, actor
Event: General Charles de Gaulle became the French prime minister, 1958

FRIDAY 2nd June — St Erasmus

LOVE: You're in a very sensitive and vulnerable state today so mind how you go.
LOOT: Make your intentions and wishes crystal clear when talking money.
LIFE: Is someone trying to undermine you or is it only in your imagination?
LUCK: ʊ

A. M: *P. M:*
Born: Marvin Hamlisch, 1944, US composer
Event: Clothes rationing began in Britain, 1941

SATURDAY 3rd June — St Charles Lwanga & Companions

LOVE: Someone surprising gives you a wonderful ego boost.
LOOT: You're attracted by a crusade, campaign or altruistic idea.
LIFE: Enlist the help or support of someone you really respect.
LUCK: ʊʊʊʊ

A. M: *P. M*:

Born: Penelope Wilton, 1947, actress
Event: The Duke of Windsor married Mrs Wallis Simpson, 1937

NOTES:

Monday 29th May
New Moon in Gemini

JUNE						
S	M	T	W	T	F	S
				1	2	3
4	5	6	7	8	9	10
11	12	13	14	15	16	17
18	19	20	21	22	23	24
25	26	27	28	29	30	

SUNDAY 4th June Pentecost — St Optatus

LOVE: Got nothing planned? Then arrange an impromptu party or gathering, pronto!
LOOT: A partner or pal shows how generous and kind they can be.
LIFE: It's difficult to get down to hard work but do your best.
LUCK: ☻

A. M: *P. M:*

Born: Geoffrey Palmer, 1927, actor
Event: Institution of the Order of the British Empire, 1917

MONDAY 5th June — St Boniface

LOVE: Talk through important topics with your other half.
LOOT: A joint account or official money matter needs careful consideration.
LIFE: You're able to tell the sheep from the goats today when dealing with colleagues.
LUCK: ☻

A. M: *P. M:*
Born: Margaret Drabble, 1939, novelist
Event: The Montgolfier brothers demonstrated the first hot-air balloon, 1783

TUESDAY 6th June — St Martha

LOVE: Try to avoid putting a dear one on a pedestal.
LOOT: A money-making scheme needs careful consideration now.
LIFE: An associate or partner isn't thinking or acting as clearly as usual.
LUCK: ☻☻☻

A. M: *P. M:*

Born: Mike Gatting, 1958, cricketer
Event: D-Day, the Allied invasion of Normandy, 1944

WEDNESDAY 7th June — St Paul of Constantinople

LOVE: You'll have a loving, affectionate and enjoyable time with loved ones.
LOOT: Splash out on a romantic meal or outing for two.
LIFE: It's a good day for discussing your feelings and needs with associates.
LUCK: ☻

A. M: *P. M:*
Born: Virginia McKenna, 1931, actress
Event: The Vatican City, Rome, was created, 1929

THURSDAY *8th June* — St William of York

LOVE: A moral dilemma or quandary teaches you volumes about yourself.
LOOT: Objects or artifacts from another country or culture appeal today.
LIFE: Give a colleague or customer the benefit of the doubt.
LUCK: ☺☺☺☺

A. M: *P. M:*

Born: Derek Underwood, 1945, cricketer
Event: The Prophet Mohammed died,632

FRIDAY *9th June* — St Columba

LOVE: A family problem you hoped had gone away starts to return from today.
LOOT: Be very careful if arranging an investment, will or large payment.
LIFE: Your confidence will either be undermined or boosted this summer.
LUCK: ☺

A. M: *P. M:*

Born: Cole Porter, 1893, US composer/lyricist
Event: The House of Commons proceedings were first broadcast live, 1975

SATURDAY *10th June* — St Bogumilus

LOVE: You may meet someone now who sweeps you straight off your feet.
LOOT: Come to a financial arrangement with your partner that suits you both.
LIFE: You need to follow your own star now and not listen to what others think.
LUCK: ☺☺☺☺

A. M: *P. M:*
Born: HRH Prince Philip, Duke of Edinburgh, 1921
Event: William Wilson & Dr Robert Smith, founded Alcoholics Anonymous in America, 1938

NOTES:

		JUNE				
S	M	T	W	T	F	S
					1	2	3
4	5	6	7	8	9	10
11	12	13	14	15	16	17
18	19	20	21	22	23	24
25	26	27	28	29	30	

SUNDAY 11th June — St Barnabas

LOVE: The closer you are to others now, the happier you'll be.
LOOT: Budgets or spending plans go for a burton today.
LIFE: Take the opportunity to get to know an associate or colleague.
LUCK: ☋

A. M: *P. M:*

Born: Jackie Stewart, 1939, champion racing driver
Event: King Henry VIII married Catherine of Aragon, 1509

MONDAY 12th June — St Leo III

LOVE: You're generous and good-hearted to everyone you meet now.
LOOT: Pecuniary matters look rosier than they've been all month.
LIFE: Wheeling and dealing or negotiations go like clockwork today.
LUCK: ☋☋☋☋

A. M: *P. M:*

Born: Anne Frank, 1929, Dutch/Jewish diarist
Event: Boris Yeltsin elected president of the new Russian Republic, 1991

TUESDAY 13th June — St Anthony of Padua

LOVE: Events that take place now will teach you a lot about the world and its ways.
LOOT: Try to adopt a new fiscal strategy that'll be easy to follow.
LIFE: If you can learn from past mistakes you'll be assured of a bright new tomorrow.
LUCK: ☋☋☋☋

A. M: *P. M:*
Born: Malcolm McDowell, 1943, actor
Event: Alexander the Great died, 323 BC

WEDNESDAY 14th June — St Dogmael

LOVE: Talk things through with a relative or loved one.
LOOT: There are repairs or renovations to be made to your abode.
LIFE: Hard work brings its own rewards today - and how!
LUCK: ☋

A. M: *P. M:*

Born: Steffi Graf, 1969, German tennis player
Event: The First Henley Regatta, 1839

THURSDAY 15th June Corpus Christi St Orsisius

LOVE: Dealing with dear ones is hard going today as they're easily upset.
LOOT: A discussion or chat sparks off a right old set-to.
LIFE: Someone challenges your ideas or proposition.
LUCK: UUU

A. M: *P. M:*

Born: Simon Callow, 1949, actor/director
Event : King John signed the Magna Carta at Runnymede, 1215

FRIDAY 16th June St Aurelian

LOVE: Why not start the weekend here, surrounded by the folk you love the most?
LOOT: Budgets or spending plans go for six today for you've got the urge to splurge!
LIFE: Bring out your creative and artistic attributes for all the world to see.
LUCK: UUUU

A. M: *P. M:*
Born: James Bolam, 1938, actor
Event: Arrest of burglars at the Democratic Party headquarters, Washington, D.C, 1972

SATURDAY 17th June St Botulph

LOVE: You're about to meet someone who makes a big impression on you.
LOOT: Treat yourself to a Saturday of enjoyment, pleasure or travel.
LIFE: Your enthusiasm for a new project or idea knows no bounds today.
LUCK: UUUU

A. M: *P. M:*

Born: Beryl Reid, 1920, actress
Event: The American War of Independence began, 1775

NOTES:

Tuesday 13th June
Full Moon in Sagittarius

JUNE

S	M	T	W	T	F	S
				1	2	3
4	5	6	7	8	9	10
11	12	13	14	15	16	17
18	19	20	21	22	23	24
25	26	27	28	29	30	

SUNDAY 18th June Father's Day St Amandus of Bordeaux

LOVE: Seek out folk who view the world from a different angle or perspective.
LOOT: Booked your holiday yet? Then start making plans pronto!
LIFE: Adopt a new strategy or take a leaf out of someone's book.
LUCK: UUU

A. M: *P. M:*

Born: Delia Smith, 1940, cookery writer
Event: General Neguib became the President of Egypt, 1953

MONDAY 19th June St Gervasius & St Protasius

LOVE: Someone takes your goodwill for granted once too often.
LOOT: A lack of service or consideration makes you mad.
LIFE: A partner or colleague steps way out of line.
LUCK: UU

A. M: *P. M:*

Born: Salman Rushdie, 1947, novelist
Event: The Royal family renounced German names and adopted the name Windsor, 1917

TUESDAY 20th June St Alban

LOVE: Restore the peace between you and a certain someone.
LOOT: You're interested in a scheme that helps others fend for themselves.
LIFE: Discussions, chats and meetings all go according to plan.
LUCK: UUUU

A. M: *P. M:*

Born: Catherine Cookson, 1906, novelist
Event: With the death of William IV, Queen Victoria ascended to the throne, 1837

WEDNESDAY 21st June St Aloysius Gonzaga

LOVE: Hidden tensions between you and an amour rise to the surface.
LOOT: Someone thinks they know best about things that are your business.
LIFE: You're about to be bathed in the spotlight of success and acclaim.
LUCK: UU

A. M: *P. M:*

Born: Prince William, 1982
Event: The laying of the foundation stone for St Paul's Cathedral, London, 1675

THURSDAY 22nd June   St Thomas More

LOVE: Invite an older chum or relative over to your place or take them out.
LOOT: You can solve pecuniary problems peacefully and productively
          now.
LIFE: Show superiors and associates that you're an asset for their team.
LUCK: ☋

A. M: P. M:

Born: Esther Rantzen, 1940, TV Presenter
Event: Celebration of the Diamond Jubilee of Queen Victoria , 1897

FRIDAY 23rd June   St Etheldreda

LOVE: Let a loved one know you won't stand being messed about.
LOOT: Invest a little shared cash in something you'll both enjoy.
LIFE: You're dynamic and determined when it comes to career matters.
LUCK: ☋

A. M: P. M:

Born: Adam Faith, 1940, singer/actor/businessman
Event: British spies, Guy Burgess & Donald Maclean, defected to the USSR, 1951

SATURDAY 24th June   St John the Baptist

LOVE: You're interested in serious rather than flighty folk today.
LOOT: Sort out a shared affair or official issue before it gets you down.
LIFE: You've no problems putting business above pleasure now.
LUCK: ☋

A. M: P. M:

Born: Jack Dempsey, 1895, heavyweight boxer
Event: Edward II was defeated at Bannockburn by Robert the Bruce, 1314

NOTES:

JUNE						
S	M	T	W	T	F	S
				1	2	3
4	5	6	7	8	9	10
11	12	13	14	15	16	17
18	19	20	21	22	23	24
25	26	27	28	29	30	

SUNDAY 25th June   St Prosper of Aquitaine

LOVE: You're annoyed by someone's greedy or grabbing ways.
LOOT: Try to keep your financial affairs private today.
LIFE: Don't be shy of saying no if you're asked to do things you object to.
LUCK: ○○○○

A. M: P. M:

Born: Carly Simon, 1945, US singer/songwriter
Event: The first Sherlock Holmes story by Arthur Conan Doyle was published, 1891

MONDAY 26th June   St Anthelmus

LOVE: A compliment or invitation really makes your day.
LOOT: Plan a pleasure trip or jaunt to a place that's near or far.
LIFE: Enlist the help of like-minded folk.
LUCK: ○○○○

A. M: P. M:

Born: Georgie Fame, 1943, singer/songwriter
Event: 50 nations signed the United Nations Charter in San Francisco, 1945

TUESDAY 27th June   St Cyril of Alexandria

LOVE: You're touched by a loved one's selfless ways.
LOOT: You understand now that not everything can be measured in terms
         of money.
LIFE: Make an effort to welcome new colleagues into the fold.
LUCK: ○

A. M: P. M:

Born: Alan Coren, 1938, author/journalist/broadcaster
Event: The United States Navy & Air Force was sent to Korea by President Truman, 1950

WEDNESDAY 28th June   St Irenaeus

LOVE: You need to establish a new understanding with an old pal.
LOOT: If you need to cut back on cash then start with status symbols.
LIFE: Grab any chance to get ahead or put your name on the map now.
LUCK: ○

A. M: P. M:

Born: John Inman, 1937, actor
Event: Queen Victoria was crowned at Westminster Abbey, 1838

THURSDAY 29th June
St Peter & St Paul

LOVE: One of the clan keeps you guessing or makes you tear your heart out.
LOOT: A recent purchase is no good or breaks down.
LIFE: Someone's daffy or daft ways drive you to distraction.
LUCK: ☽

A. M: *P. M*:

Born: Nelson Eddy, 1901, US film actor/singer
Event: Shakespeare's Globe theatre was burned down, 1613

FRIDAY 30th June
St Bertrand of Le Mans

LOVE: You have to think again now about a particular partnership.
LOOT: Sort out money tangles before they tie you in knots.
LIFE: Flaws or failings are disheartening but point you in the right direction.
LUCK: ☽☽☽☽

A. M: *P. M*:

Born: Mike Tyson, 1966, US heavyweight boxer
Event: Parliament abolished the use of the pillory, 1837

SATURDAY 1st July
St Oliver Plunket

LOVE: Arrange an outing with your best pal and enjoy yourselves.
LOOT: A trip or away-day is just what you need.
LIFE: Broaden your horizons about your hopes for the future.
LUCK: ☽☽

A. M: *P. M*:

Born: HRH the Princess of Wales, 1961
Event: The Jacobites were defeated by William III at the battle of the Boyne, 1690

NOTES:

Wednesday 28th June
New Moon in Cancer

		JULY				
S	M	T	W	T	F	S
						1
2	3	4	5	6	7	8
9	10	11	12	13	14	15
16	17	18	19	20	21	22
23	24	25	26	27	28	29
30	31					

SUNDAY 2nd July — St Monegundis

LOVE: A so-called pal tries to trip you up.
LOOT: Keep friends and finances far apart today.
LIFE: A future plan hits a hitch that needs careful handling.
LUCK: ☽

A. M: *P. M:*

Born: Hermann Hesse, 1877, German poet/novelist
Event: Nostradamus the astrologer died, 1566

MONDAY 3rd July — St Anatolius

LOVE: You're horrified at someone's discriminatory or divisive tactics.
LOOT: If plans have been made behind your back you'll be furious now.
LIFE: An arrangement or campaign comes under fire.
LUCK: ☽☽☽

A. M: *P. M:*

Born: Tom Stoppard, 1937, playwright
Event: The first television transmission by John Logie Baird, 1928

TUESDAY 4th July — St Andrew of Crete

LOVE: Whatever anyone says you'll rise to the attack.
LOOT: A fiscal affair gets your goat but is it really that important?
LIFE: You'll work hard now but may get little reward for your pains.
LUCK: ☽

A. M: *P. M:*

Born: Gina Lollobrigida, 1927, Italian film actress
Event: The people of France presented the Statue of Liberty to the USA, 1883

WEDNESDAY 5th July — St Anthony Zaccaria

LOVE: A difficult relative or dear one can be coaxed into line now.
LOOT: An older pal or advisor has some good ideas this July.
LIFE: Make an effort to win the support of people in power this month.
LUCK: ☽☽☽☽

A. M: *P. M:*

Born: Jean Cocteau, 1889, French poet/novelist/artist
Event: The National Health Service started, 1948

THURSDAY 6th July   St Maria Goretti

LOVE: If you've been at someone's beck and call then the worm's about to turn!
LOOT: Start to scrutinise all daily outgoings and see where to cut back.
LIFE: Events will prove whether or not a job is right for you this summer.
LUCK: ∪∪

A. M: P. M:

Born: Geraldine James, 1950, actress
Event: Thomas More was executed, 1535

FRIDAY 7th July   St Palladius

LOVE: Take care or someone will knock the wind out of your sails.
LOOT: A forthcoming trip or jaunt turns out to cost more than you thought.
LIFE: You have to deal with a colleagues ungenerous or critical words.
LUCK: ∪∪

A. M: P. M:

Born: Bill Oddie, 1941, comedian/ornithologist
Event: Christopher Stone presented the first gramophone record programme to be broadcast by the BBC, 1927

SATURDAY 8th July   St Kilian

LOVE: Visit or phone someone from a different generation.
LOOT: Try to mind your own business if a parent or pal seems extravagant.
LIFE: Talk to bosses or power brokers about what you want.
LUCK: ∪

A. M: P. M:

Born: Brian Walden, 1932, journalist/broadcaster
Event: The Ziegfeld Follies opened in New York, 1907

NOTES:

		JULY				
S	M	T	W	T	F	S
						1
2	3	4	5	6	7	8
9	10	11	12	13	14	15
16	17	18	19	20	21	22
23	24	25	26	27	28	29
30	31					

SUNDAY 9th July   St Veronica de Julianis

LOVE: One of the clan seems stuck in a rut or locked in the past.
LOOT: Buy something unusual or different for your dwelling.
LIFE: Let your ideas flow and boost your confidence in yourself.
LUCK: ひひひひ

A. M: *P. M:*

Born: Michael Williams, 1935, actor
Event: Independence of the Bahamas, 1973

MONDAY 10th July   St Amelberga

LOVE: A parent, mentor or older chum has important news in the next
            fortnight.
LOOT: Slice through red tape now or apply for promotion.
LIFE: Want to improve your qualifications? Then get cracking now.
LUCK: ひ

A. M: *P. M:*

Born: Arthur Ashe, 1943, tennis player
Event: Lady Jane Grey proclaimed Queen of England, 1553

TUESDAY 11th July   St Benedict

LOVE: Dealings with one of the clan give you food for thought.
LOOT: If you give money to a relative then keep it between the two of you.
LIFE: You're happy to give credit where credit's due today.
LUCK: ひ

A. M: *P. M:*

Born: John Stride, 1936, actor
Event: The last voyage of Captain Cook, 1776

WEDNESDAY 12th July   St John Gualbert

LOVE: A domestic dilemma of difficulty needs resolving, pronto.
LOOT: Important news is on the way about your abode or family finances.
LIFE: You'll need the patience of a saint where workaday dealings are
            concerned.
LUCK: ひ

A. M: *P. M:*

Born: Jennifer Saunders, 1958, comedienne/actress
Event: Cyprus came under British rule, 1878

THURSDAY 13th July   St Henry II

LOVE: One of the clan gets uppity or tries to upset the apple cart.
LOOT: A domestic bill or expense causes raised eyebrows all round.
LIFE: It's hard to concentrate or keep your mind on the job today.
LUCK: ☾☾☾☾

A. M: *P. M:*

Born: Harrison Ford, 1942, US actor
Event: Jean-Paul Marat was murdered in his bath by Charlotte Corday, 1793

FRIDAY 14th July   St Camillus of Lellis

LOVE: The generation gap counts for nowt where affection's concerned
       this July.
LOOT: You're realising that money and happiness don't always go hand in
       hand.
LIFE: You're in the driving seat when it comes to career issues now.
LUCK: ☾

A. M: *P. M:*
Born: Sue Lawley, 1946, TV and radio presenter
Event: The storming of the Bastille during the French revolution,1789

SATURDAY 15th July   St Bonaventure

LOVE: A woman proves what a friend she is.
LOOT: Have a pow-wow about forthcoming decisions that affect the whole
       tribe.
LIFE: Discussions and meetings go like clockwork.
LUCK: ☾☾☾

A. M: *P. M:*

Born: Linda Ronstadt, 1946, US singer
Event: Founding of Alcoholics Anonymous in Britain, 1948

NOTES:

Wednesday 12th July
Full Moon in Capricorn

JULY						
S	M	T	W	T	F	S
						1
2	3	4	5	6	7	8
9	10	11	12	13	14	15
16	17	18	19	20	21	22
23	24	25	26	27	28	29
30	31					

SUNDAY 16th July   St Eustathius

LOVE: Seek the peace if you've fallen out with a relative or friend.
LOOT: Someone's suggestions or hints are well worth listening to.
LIFE: A project gets the green light or seal of approval.
LUCK: ☋

A. M: *P. M:*

Born: Ginger Rogers, 1911, film actress/dancer
Event: Nicholas II and family were murdered by the Bolsheviks, 1918

MONDAY 17th July   St Ennodius

LOVE: Someone's foggy, fuzzy and woolly ways set your teeth on edge.
LOOT: Steer clear of all deals and commitments today.
LIFE: Does a boss know what they want? You're beginning to doubt it.
LUCK: ☋☋☋☋

A. M: *P. M:*

Born: Donald Sutherland, 1935, US film actor
Event: The opening of Disneyland in California, 1955

TUESDAY 18th July   St Arnulf

LOVE: One-to-one affairs are super - just the way you like them!
LOOT: A partner sounds a warning but are they over-reacting?
LIFE: Interviews, appointments and meetings all go with a swing.
LUCK: ☋☋

A. M: *P. M:*

Born: Nelson Mandela, 1918, South African politician
Event: The formal opening of the Mersey Tunnel, 1934

WEDNESDAY 19th July   St Macrina

LOVE: A close companion is restless, rude, impatient or impossible.
LOOT: An unexpected expense sends you on the rampage.
LIFE: Toeing the line or abiding by the rules is like a red rag to a bull.
LUCK: ☋

A. M: *P. M:*

Born: George Hamilton IV, 1937, US Country singer
Event: The first Wimbledon Men's Singles Tennis final, 1877

THURSDAY 20th July   St Aurelius

LOVE: The years that separate you and someone special mean nothing now.
LOOT: Listen carefully to someone's advice or suggestion.
LIFE: Bosses and superiors find you very impressive indeed today.
LUCK: ☍

A. M: P. M:

Born: Diana Rigg, 1938, actress
Event: The US space probe, Viking I, landed on Mars, 1975

FRIDAY 21st July   St Lawrence of Brindisi

LOVE: Someone you respect shows a very different side to their nature.
LOOT: There's an untimely reminder about a debt or payment.
LIFE: Even the best laid plans could go on the blink today.
LUCK: ☍

A. M: P. M:

Born: Ernest Hemingway, 1899, US novelist
Event: Neil Armstrong was the first man on the moon, 1969

SATURDAY 22nd July   St Mary Magdalene

LOVE: You're fast and furious in all personal affairs but don't trip yourself up.
LOOT: You'll find it hard to restrain your spending this summer.
LIFE: Put your best foot forward and seize the initiative now!
LUCK: ☍☍☍

A. M: P. M:

Born: Terence Stamp, 1938, actor
Event: The first round the world solo flight was completed by Wiley Post, 1933

NOTES:

JULY						
S	M	T	W	T	F	S
						1
2	3	4	5	6	7	8
9	10	11	12	13	14	15
16	17	18	19	20	21	22
23	24	25	26	27	28	29
30	31					

SUNDAY 23rd July — St Apollinaris

LOVE: Join a new club, gang or society this month or get together with friends.

LOOT: Splash out on a hobby or activity that you really enjoy.

LIFE: Concentrate your efforts on pushing ahead with schemes and dreams.

LUCK: ☾☾☾

A. M: P. M:

Born: Raymond Chandler, 1888, US novelist
Event: John Dunlop applied for a patent for a pneumatic tyre, 1888

MONDAY 24th July — St Boris of Romanus

LOVE: A loved one is hard to please or too exacting for comfort.

LOOT: It seems you need to tighten your belt over household bills.

LIFE: Someone's high standards are hard to live up to.

LUCK: ☾

A. M: P. M:

Born: Amelia Earhart, 1898, US aviator
Event: Antoine de la Mothe Cadillac founded the city of Detroit in America, 1701

TUESDAY 25th July — St Christopher

LOVE: A chat with a relative or pal lets you both know where you stand.

LOOT: Talk to folk in the know about increasing your income.

LIFE: Do what's expected of you now and enjoy the compliments.

LUCK: ☾☾

A. M: P. M:

Born: Lynne Frederick, 1954, actress
Event: Birth of the first test-tube baby in Oldham, Lancs, 1978

WEDNESDAY 26th July — St Anne & St Joachim

LOVE: Social settings and group gatherings are grist to your mill.

LOOT: You'll spot the very thing you need for a pastime or hobby.

LIFE: Enlist someone's help in pushing forward with future plans.

LUCK: ☾

A. M: P. M:

Born: Helen Mirren, 1946, actress
Event: Inauguration of the Federal Bureau of Investigation, 1908

THURSDAY 27th July — St Pantaleon

LOVE: Someone's intense emotions catch you on the hop.
LOOT: A red-letter day for negotiations and signing contracts.
LIFE: You're about to get the help you need over a pet project.
LUCK: ᴜᴜᴜᴜ

A. M: P. M:

Born: Jack Higgins, 1929, novelist
Event: The first time a radio compass was used to navigate aircraft, 1920

FRIDAY 28th July — St Innocent

LOVE: Someone tries to shock you - and succeeds admirably!
LOOT: Loot's leaking out through a hole in your budget.
LIFE: Don't count your chickens before they're hatched today.
LUCK: ᴜᴜᴜᴜ

A. M: P. M:

Born: Jacqueline Onassis, 1929
Event: The first potatoes were brought to England from Colombia, 1586

SATURDAY 29th July — St Lupus

LOVE: Parties, picnics, gala outings or gregarious get-togethers see you shine now.
LOOT: Why not enrol in that club, group or society that you've always wanted to join?
LIFE: Start oiling the wheels or paving the way for a cherished plan.
LUCK: ᴜᴜᴜᴜ

A. M: P. M:
Born: Diane Keen, 1946, actress
Event: The Prince of Wales married Lady Diana Spencer, 1981

NOTES:

Thursday 27th July
New Moon in Leo

JULY						
S	M	T	W	T	F	S
						1
2	3	4	5	6	7	8
9	10	11	12	13	14	15
16	17	18	19	20	21	22
23	24	25	26	27	28	29
30	31					

SUNDAY 30th July St Peter Chrysologus

LOVE: A blank day in your diary? Then make some plans, pronto!
LOOT: You'll be delighted with what you buy today.
LIFE: Explain your ideas and schemes and folk will sit up and take notice.
LUCK: UUUU

A. M: *P. M:*

Born: Henry Moore, 1898, sculptor
Event: The Football World cup was won by England at Wembley, 1966

MONDAY 31st July St Giovanni Colombini

LOVE: A sweetheart's in a bad mood and determined to take it out on you.
LOOT: There's bad or discouraging news today.
LIFE: Someone drags their heels or won't commit themselves.
LUCK: U

A. M: *P. M:*

Born: Geraldine Chaplin, 1944, US film actress
Event: Dr Crippen was arrested for the murder of his wife, 1910

TUESDAY 1st August St Alphonsus Liguori

LOVE: You realise how much a particular pal means to you today.
LOOT: Treat yourself to something for your favourite hobby or interest.
LIFE: Steer a pet project back on to the road to success.
LUCK: UU

A. M: *P. M:*

Born: Yves Saint Laurent, 1936, French haute couturier
Event: Admiral Lord Nelson destroyed the French Fleet at the Battle of the Nile, 1798

WEDNESDAY 2nd August St Eusebius of Vercelli

LOVE: Why not widen your interests and social circle at the same time?
LOOT: Think about updating or improving your mode of transport.
LIFE: The more contact you have with others, the better you'll fare now.
LUCK: UUUU

A. M: *P. M:*

Born: Alan Whicker, 1925, TV broadcaster
Event: The US Marshall 'Wild Bill' Hickok was shot dead, 1876

THURSDAY 3rd August — St Germanus of Auxerre

LOVE: Head for the nearest party or gathering - who knows who you may meet?
LOOT: Boodle's burning a hole in your pocket.
LIFE: A super day for making some very influential friends.
LUCK: UUU

A. M:

P. M:

Born: PD James, 1920, authoress
Event: The first ship sailed through the Panama Canal, 1914

FRIDAY 4th August — St Jean-Baptiste Vianney

LOVE: You're doubtful about a loved one's motives or morals.
LOOT: Keep a big distance between money and friends today.
LIFE: Someone's full of promises but will they do what they say?
LUCK: UU

A. M:

P. M:

Born: HM Queen Elizabeth, the Queen Mother, 1900
Event: Britain declared war on Germany, 1914

SATURDAY 5th August — St Addai & St Mari

LOVE: You're thrilled to accept an invitation or suggestion.
LOOT: Heading for the shops? Well, don't get carried away!
LIFE: Put your ideas across and forget about false modesty.
LUCK: UUUU

A. M:

P. M:

Born: Joan Hickson, 1906, actress
Event: Abolition of Polygamy in Turkey, 1924

NOTES:

AUGUST

S	M	T	W	T	F	S
		1	*2*	*3*	*4*	*5*
6	*7*	*8*	*9*	*10*	*11*	*12*
13	*14*	*15*	*16*	*17*	*18*	*19*
20	*21*	*22*	*23*	*24*	*25*	*26*
27	*28*	*29*	*30*	*31*		

SUNDAY 6th August · St Hormisdas

LOVE: A friend really makes your day.
LOOT: You spot just the thing for a pet interest or pastime.
LIFE: A social setting introduces you to influential folk.
LUCK: ☾☾☾

A. M: *P. M*:

Born: Barbara Windsor, 1937, actress
Event: Independence of Jamaica, 1962

MONDAY 7th August · St Cajetan

LOVE: A chat with a chum is revealing and rewarding.
LOOT: Take yourself off for a wee trip or pleasure jaunt.
LIFE: You'll make good progress in a hope for the future.
LUCK: ☾☾

A. M: *P. M*:

Born: Nick Ross, 1947, journalist/broadcaster
Event: Act of Parliament passed to prohibit the employment of boys as chimney sweeps, 1840

TUESDAY 8th August · St Dominic

LOVE: Someone undermines your confidence or stirs up guilty feelings.
LOOT: A house move or big purchase is about to revolutionise your life!
LIFE: A cherished plan or hope is blocked through spite or jealousy.
LUCK: ☾☾

A. M: *P. M*:

Born: Nigel Mansell, 1953, racing driver
Event: £2,500,000 was stolen in the Great Train Robbery, 1963

WEDNESDAY 9th August · St Mattias

LOVE: Events reveal the significance someone plays in your life.
LOOT: Financial affairs need pruning, purging, refining or rethinking.
LIFE: Someone has a dramatic impact on you from today.
LUCK: ☾☾

A. M: *P. M*:

Born: Philip Larkin, 1922, Poet
Event: The border between the USA and Canada was recognised, 1842

THURSDAY 10th August   St Laurence

LOVE: A loving liaison goes from strength to strength.
LOOT: It's time to cut your coat according to your cloth.
LIFE: Put the finishing touches to a project or you'll miss the boat.
LUCK: ☽☽☽☽

A. M: *P. M:*

Born: Kate O'Mara, 1939, actress
Event: The British Parliament voted to receive salaries (£400 per year), 1911

FRIDAY 11th August   St Clare

LOVE: You'll hear a secret soon, but can you keep it to yourself?
LOOT: Seek help now if you can't make the money go round.
LIFE: An offer takes you by surprise or arrives when least expected.
LUCK: ☽☽

A. M: *P. M:*

Born: Enid Blyton, 1897, authoress
Event: King Hussein of Jordan succeeded to the throne, 1952

SATURDAY 12th August   St Euplus

LOVE: Who'd have thought it? You hear something surprising today.
LOOT: Your earning power is on the increase now.
LIFE: You've got more clout than you realise, so stick your neck out!
LUCK: ☽☽☽

A. M: *P. M:*

Born: Michael Brunson, 1940, TV reporter/newscaster
Event: The first communications satellite, Echo I, was launched, 1960

NOTES:

Thursday 10th August
Full Moon in Aquarius

AUGUST						
S	M	T	W	T	F	S
		1	2	3	4	5
6	7	8	9	10	11	12
13	14	15	16	17	18	19
20	21	22	23	24	25	26
27	28	29	30	31		

SUNDAY 13th August — St Maximus

LOVE: An invitation or proposal raises your eyebrows.
LOOT: You're on top form when it comes to negotiations.
LIFE: Don't overlook loose ends or the small print.
LUCK: ☾☾☾

A. M: *P. M:*

Born: Madhur Jaffrey, 1933, actress/cookery writer
Event: The Austrians and English defeated the French at Blenheim, 1704

MONDAY 14th August — St Maximilian Kolbe

LOVE: One-to-one affairs are more like pitched battles today.
LOOT: Someone's annoyed you but they won't let you say so.
LIFE: Partners are quick to fly off the handle or deflect the flak.
LUCK: ☾

A. M: *P. M:*

Born: Frederick Raphael, 1931, novelist
Event: Queen Victoria received the Zulu Chief Cetewayo at Osborne, 1882

TUESDAY 15th August — St Arnulf

LOVE: Dealings with dear ones return to normal today.
LOOT: You need to consider a partner's future finances.
LIFE: Partners and pals help you understand yourself.
LUCK: ☾☾

A. M: *P. M:*

Born: Oscar Peterson, 1925, Jazz pianist
Event: The King of Scotland, Macbeth, killed in battle, 1057

WEDNESDAY 16th August — St Roch

LOVE: Increase your social circle or join a new club or group.
LOOT: Put your money where your mouth is!
LIFE: Grab every opportunity now to push your ideas forward.
LUCK: ☾☾

A. M: *P. M:*

Born: Madonna, 1958, US rock singer
Event: The opening of the Tate Gallery in London, 1897

THURSDAY 17th August — St Hyacinth

LOVE: You're called on to make a sacrifice.
LOOT: Help someone who's broke without hurting their pride.
LIFE: The lessons you learn today stand you in good stead for the future.
LUCK: U

A. M:

P. M:

Born: Robert de Niro, 1943, US film actor
Event: The Registration Act was introduced for all births, deaths & marriages, 1836

FRIDAY 18th August — St Agapitus

LOVE: Can you really believe what a loved one is telling you?
LOOT: A pipe-dream needs a sudden injection of cash.
LIFE: You have to make a tricky decision.
LUCK: UU

A. M:

P. M:

Born: Shelley Winters, 1922, US film actress
Event: Genghis Khan died, 1227

SATURDAY 19th August — St John Eudes

LOVE: A partner tries to tie you down or acts unreasonably.
LOOT: You have to compromise your ideals or beliefs.
LIFE: Is someone saying things behind your back?
LUCK: UU

A. M:

P. M:

Born: Coco Chanel, 1883, French fashion designer
Event: Groucho Marx died, 1977

NOTES:

AUGUST

S	M	T	W	T	F	S
		1	*2*	*3*	*4*	*5*
6	*7*	*8*	*9*	*10*	*11*	*12*
13	*14*	*15*	*16*	*17*	*18*	*19*
20	*21*	*22*	*23*	*24*	*25*	*26*
27	*28*	*29*	*30*	*31*		

SUNDAY 20th August   St Bernard

LOVE: You're in an expansive and sociable mood.
LOOT: Buy anything that increases your knowledge of the world.
LIFE: Someone gives you their full support.
LUCK: ∪∪

A. M: *P. M:*

Born: Robert Plant, 1948, rock singer
Event: Fighting broke out in Prague as Russian troops invaded Czechoslovakia, 1968

MONDAY 21st August   St Jane Frances de Chantel

LOVE: A so-called friend shows their true colours.
LOOT: Keep money and mates as far apart as possible.
LIFE: A partner throws a giant spanner in the works.
LUCK: ∪

A. M: *P. M:*

Born: HRH Princess Margaret, 1930
Event: Leonardo da Vinci's *Mona Lisa* was stolen from the Louvre, 1911

TUESDAY 22nd August   St Andrew of Fiesole

LOVE: There's just no pleasing some folk today.
LOOT: Someone jumps down your throat or is deliberately rude.
LIFE: A boss or superior is flexing their muscles at your expense.
LUCK: ∪

A. M: *P. M:*

Born: Steve Davis, 1957, snooker player
Event: Beginning of Civil War in England, 1642

WEDNESDAY 23rd August   St Rose of Lima

LOVE: Amour is wrapped in mystery, privacy or secrecy in the month
         ahead.
LOOT: Strapped for cash? Then seek professional help and advice, pronto.
LIFE: You'll be happiest tucked away from the madding crowd now.
LUCK: ∪∪

A. M: *P. M:*

Born: Gene Kelly, 1912, US dancer/singer
Event: The Italian-born film actor, Rudolph Valentino, died, 1926

THURSDAY 24th August   St Bartholomew

LOVE: A very surprising person reveals their very soft spot for you.
LOOT: Ideal for buying things that make your abode extra cosy and serene.
LIFE: A charitable or altruistic cause brings out your protective instincts.
LUCK: UU

A. M: *P. M:*

Born: Sir Max Beerbohm, 1872, author/caricaturist
Event: Volcano, Vesuvius, erupted and buried Pompeii and Herculaneum, AD79

FRIDAY 25th August   St Joseph Calasanctius

LOVE: Social settings are just what the doctor ordered today!
LOOT: How about arranging a party or gregarious gathering?
LIFE: Grasp the nettle over a future hope or dream.
LUCK: UU

A. M: *P. M:*

Born: Sean Connery, 1930, film actor
Event: Daily scheduled flights between London and Paris began, 1919

SATURDAY 26th August   St Zephyrinus

LOVE: A secret fan is about to declare themselves!
LOOT: Keep pecuniary plans under your hat in the next fortnight.
LIFE: You make a spiritual or philosophical discovery now.
LUCK: UU

A. M: *P. M:*

Born: Christopher Isherwood, 1904, novelist
Event: Julius Caesar landed in Britain, 55 BC

NOTES:

Saturday 26th August
New Moon in Virgo

AUGUST						
S	M	T	W	T	F	S
		1	2	3	4	5
6	7	8	9	10	11	12
13	14	15	16	17	18	19
20	21	22	23	24	25	26
27	28	29	30	31		

SUNDAY 27th August St Caesarius

LOVE: A dear one sends you on a wild goose chase.
LOOT: Money worries loom large and undermine your confidence.
LIFE: You're beset by doubts or feelings of inadequacy.
LUCK: U

A. M: *P. M:*

Born: Mother Teresa, 1910, missionary
Event: Earl Mountbatten of Burma was murdered by the IRA, 1979

MONDAY 28th August Bank Holiday St Augustine of Hippo

LOVE: A longed-for invitation or request arrives at last!
LOOT: Buy yourself a little treat or luxury.
LIFE: A charitable or community concern goes like a dream.
LUCK: UUUU

A. M: *P. M:*

Born: Emlyn Hughes, 1947, footballer
Event: 200,000 black Americans demonstrate civil rights in Washington DC, 1963

TUESDAY 29th August St Sabina of Rome

LOVE: You're eloquent, articulate and loquacious between now and November.
LOOT: A marvellous time for sorting out money matters.
LIFE: Take the initiative in all personal projects from today.
LUCK: UUUU

A. M: *P. M:*

Born: Lenny Henry, 1958, comedian
Event: Founding of the city of Melbourne, Australia, 1835

WEDNESDAY 30th August St Pammachius

LOVE: Be brave and make the first move towards a prospective paramour!
LOOT: Only spend money you know you've got today.
LIFE: A little gamble or speculation has unforeseen advantages.
LUCK: UUUU

A. M: *P. M:*

Born: Fred MacMurray, 1908, US film actor
Event: The Queen of Egypt, Cleopatra, committed suicide, 30 BC

THURSDAY 31st August   St Aidan

LOVE: You'll welcome someone surprising into your life now.
LOOT: A good day for balancing your needs with your spending power.
LIFE: An altruistic or spiritual pursuit really appeals now.
LUCK: ☾☾☾

A. M: *P. M:*

Born: Van Morrison, 1945, rock singer
Event: The first victim of Jack the Ripper was found dead in Whitechapel London, 1888

FRIDAY 1st September   St Giles

LOVE: Something from your past solves a current problem.
LOOT: Buy things that update or beautify your abode.
LIFE: The moods of dear ones rub off on you today.
LUCK: ☾☾

A. M: *P. M:*

Born: Lilly Tomlin, 1939, US TV entertainer
Event: The Cape of Good Hope issued the first triangular postage stamps, 1853

SATURDAY 2nd September   St John the Faster

LOVE: Sort out a family problem before it gets any worse.
LOOT: Is there no way out of your current money maze?
LIFE: Alter anything that no longer fits into your world.
LUCK: ☾☾☾☾

A. M: *P. M:*

Born: Jimmy Connors, 1952, tennis player
Event: The Great Fire of London started, 1666

NOTES:

SEPTEMBER						
S	M	T	W	T	F	S
					1	2
3	4	5	6	7	8	9
10	11	12	13	14	15	16
17	18	19	20	21	22	23
24	25	26	27	28	29	30

SUNDAY 3rd September — St Gregory the Great

LOVE: You're in complete accord with the folk around you now.
LOOT: Had a holiday yet? Then arrange a break, pronto!
LIFE: A community or neighbourhood scheme finds you on fine form.
LUCK: ☾☾☾☾

A. M: P. M:

Born: Pauline Collins, 1940, actress
Event: The Gregorian Calendar replaces the Julian Calendar, 1752

MONDAY 4th September — St Boniface

LOVE: A blast from the past makes you smile.
LOOT: An old possession could be more valuable than you think.
LIFE: You realise there's more to life than meets the eye now.
LUCK: ☾☾

A. M: P. M:

Born: Dinsdale Landen, 1932, actor
Event: HM Queen opens the Forth Road Bridge, 1964

TUESDAY 5th September — St Zacharias

LOVE: Don't automatically assume that loved ones are out to get you.
LOOT: You're feeling defensive and touchy about boodle.
LIFE: Say what's wrong but don't nag or niggle needlessly.
LUCK: ☾☾

A. M: P. M:

Born: Raquel Welsh, 140, US actress
Event: Arab terrorists killed 11 Israelis at the Olympic Games in Germany, 1972

WEDNESDAY 6th September — St Cagnoald

LOVE: Tell someone exactly why they're so special.
LOOT: Super for pleasure trips or entertaining outings.
LIFE: Events that happen today lift your heart and raise your spirits.
LUCK: ☾☾☾

A. M: P. M:

Born: Britt Ekland, 1943, film actress
Event: The Great Fire of London ended, 1666

THURSDAY 7th September   St Cloud

LOVE: You're ardent and affectionate now but don't add jealousy to the list.
LOOT: It's hard to save for you'd rather spend your cash now.
LIFE: Keep in touch with your feelings but don't let them get the better of you.
LUCK: ʊʊ

A. M: *P. M:*
Born: Buddy Holly, 1936, US rock singer
Event: Grace Darling rescued the crew of stricken steam ship, *Forfarshire*, 1838

FRIDAY 8th September   St Adrian & St Natalia

LOVE: If you've got something to say then speak up today!
LOOT: You're tempted by the urge to splurge, but will you resist it?
LIFE: Put your money where your mouth is now.
LUCK: ʊʊʊʊ

A. M: *P. M*:

Born: Anne Diamond, 1954, TV presenter
Event: Richard Nixon was granted a full pardon by President Ford, 1974

SATURDAY 9th September   St Peter Claver

LOVE: A loved one takes advantage of you once too often.
LOOT: Is someone's sob story just a bid for boodle?
LIFE: Your working world needs rethinking and changing for the better.
LUCK: ʊʊ

A. M: *P. M*:

Born: Michael Aldridge, 1920, actor
Event: The Scots were defeated by the English at the battle of Flodden Field, 1513

NOTES:

Saturday 9th September
Full Moon in Pisces

SEPTEMBER						
S	M	T	W	T	F	S
					1	2
3	4	5	6	7	8	9
10	11	12	13	14	15	16
17	18	19	20	21	22	23
24	25	26	27	28	29	30

SUNDAY 10th September — St Finnian

LOVE: Is a dear one spinning you a line or leading you on?
LOOT: Try to take someone's promises with a pinch of salt.
LIFE: A super day for beautifying your garden or abode.
LUCK: ♉♉♉♉

A. M: *P. M:*

Born: Gwen Watford, 1927, actress
Event: The first German autobahn was opened, 1921

MONDAY 11th September — St Deiniol

LOVE: A partner's emotional demands are impossible to meet.
LOOT: You may not act as rationally as you think today.
LIFE: If you've got something to say then don't be shy. Speak up!
LUCK: ♉

A. M: *P, M:*

Born: Barry Sheene, 1950, racing motorcyclist
Event: The French were defeated by the Duke of Marlborough's forces, 1709

TUESDAY 12th September — St Ailbhe

LOVE: Folk are as prickly as a porcupine today. But why?
LOOT: A household bill or account starts an uproar.
LIFE: Try to keep your cool and don't rise to someone's bait.
LUCK: ♉♉

A. M: *P. M:*

Born: Ian Holme, 1931, actor
Event: Cleopatra's needle was erected in London on the Thames Embankment, 1878

WEDNESDAY 13th September — St John Chrysostom

LOVE: A super bolt from the blue leaves you speechless with surprise.
LOOT: Bored with your abode? Then give it a new image now.
LIFE: If life lacks lustre then you can inject some excitement now.
LUCK: ♉♉

A. M: *P. M:*

Born: John Smith MP, 1938
Event: New York becomes the capital of the newly formed USA, 1788

THURSDAY *14th September*   St Maternus of Cologne

LOVE: A special someone earns a big place in your heart.
LOOT: A good day to make big or important investments.
LIFE: Circumstances help you put your priorities in order.
LUCK: ℧℧

A. M: *P. M:*

Born: Jack Hawkins, 1910, film actor
Event: Napoleon and the French army entered Moscow, 1812

FRIDAY *15th September*   St Catherine of Genoa

LOVE: Someone shows the better side of their nature.
LOOT: You're fascinated by things with a spiritual slant.
LIFE: Spread your wings, whether physically or mentally.
LUCK: ℧℧℧

A. M: *P. M:*

Born: Freddie Mercury, 1946, rock singer
Event: Traffic Wardens went on duty for the first time in London, 1960

SATURDAY *16th September*   St Abundius & St Abundantius

LOVE: Your popularity's rising at a rate of knots - you star, you!
LOOT: You're anxious to help a needy or sorry soul.
LIFE: Life has a vivacious, frothy and flirtatious feel from today.
LUCK: ℧℧℧℧

A. M: *P. M:*

Born: Lauren Bacall, 1924, US actress
Event: Lake Nyasa was discovered by David Livingstone, 1859

NOTES:

SEPTEMBER						
S	M	T	W	T	F	S
					1	2
3	4	5	6	7	8	9
10	11	12	13	14	15	16
17	18	19	20	21	22	23
24	25	26	27	28	29	30

SUNDAY 17th September — St Robert Bellarmine

LOVE: The milk of human kindness flows through you today.
LOOT: A visit or jaunt sets you up for the week ahead.
LIFE: You're feeling on the sentimental side now.
LUCK: ☺☺☺☺

A. M: *P. M:*

Born: Dinah Sheridan, 1920, actress
Event: A demonstration for long playing records was given in New York, 1931

MONDAY 18th September — St Ferreolus of Limoges

LOVE: A loved one needs a wee talking-to.
LOOT: It's a terrific day for deals, negotiations and bargaining.
LIFE: People in power are impressed by the trail you blaze today.
LUCK: ☺☺

A. M: *P. M:*

Born: Greta Garbo, 1905, Swedish actress
Event: First publication of the New York Times, 1851

TUESDAY 19th September — St Januarius

LOVE: Someone confides in you or lets you into a secret.
LOOT: Talk to influential folk about a grant, bursary or benefit.
LIFE: Consider your goals in life - are they still right for you?
LUCK: ☺☺

A. M: *P. M:*

Born: Michael Elphick, 1946, actor
Event: Melville Reuben Bissell, inventor, patented the first carpet-sweeper, 1876

WEDNESDAY 20th September — St Agapetus

LOVE: A surprising someone reveals a new side to themselves.
LOOT: You're tempted by things you wouldn't normally look at.
LIFE: Life throws up radical changes today.
LUCK: ☺☺

A. M: *P. M:*

Born: Sophia Loren, 1934, Italian film actress
Event: The launch of the liner, SS Mauretania, 1906

THURSDAY 21st September   St Matthew

LOVE: A very special person needs a shoulder to cry on.
LOOT: Go on, buy yourself a little luxury or treat!
LIFE: A private or secret matter needs sorting out.
LUCK: ƱƱ

A. M: *P. M*:

Born: Jimmy Young, 1923, Radio presenter
Event: Stonehenge was sold for £6,600 at auction, 1915

FRIDAY 22nd September   St Bodo

LOVE: Personal affairs hit hitches or blips from today.
LOOT: Don't commit yourself to anything you can't cancel now.
LIFE: Expect setbacks or muddles in the next three weeks.
LUCK: ƱƱ

A. M: *P. M*:

Born: William Franklyn, 1926, actor
Event: Independent Television started broadcasting in Britain, 1955

SATURDAY 23rd September   St Adamnan

LOVE: Expect your popularity to rise and rise in the coming month!
LOOT: Treat yourself to an outing or pleasure trip today.
LIFE: Your personality starts to sparkle and shine now.
LUCK: ƱƱƱƱ

A. M: *P. M*:

Born: Ray Charles, 1930, R&B singer/musician
Event: The planet Neptune was discovered by Johann Gottfried Galle, 1846

NOTES:

SEPTEMBER						
S	M	T	W	T	F	S
					1	2
3	4	5	6	7	8	9
10	11	12	13	14	15	16
17	18	19	20	21	22	23
24	25	26	27	28	29	30

SUNDAY 24th September — St Gerard of Csanad

LOVE: A loving liaison takes off or gets deeper from today.
LOOT: Go on, spend some money gilding the lily that is you!
LIFE: Today marks the start of a vital new phase in your life.
LUCK: ○○○○○

A. M: *P. M:*

Born: Linda McCartney, 1941, musician/photographer
Event: *The Robe*, had its world premiere in Hollywood, 1953

MONDAY 25th September — St Sergius of Rostov

LOVE: What a day! You're looking glamourous and feeling amorous!
LOOT: Go on, treat yourself to a little luxury or two - or three!
LIFE: You'll attract plenty of admiring glances today.
LUCK: ○○○○

A. M: *P. M:*

Born: Felicity Kendall, 1946, actress
Event: The opening of the Royal Court Theatre, London, 1888

TUESDAY 26th September — St Cosmas & St Damian

LOVE: Your feelings for someone go up and down like a Yo-Yo.
LOOT: Don't commit yourself to anything expensive today.
LIFE: You may not be seeing things as clearly as you imagine now.
LUCK: ○

A. M: *P. M:*

Born: George Gershwin, 1898, US composer
Event: New Zealand was proclaimed a Dominion, 1907

WEDNESDAY 27th September — St Frumentius

LOVE: Ouch! A loved one finds the chink in your armour.
LOOT: Proceed with considerable caution in all cash concerns.
LIFE: It's hard to tell the difference between advice and criticism today.
LUCK: ○

A. M: *P. M:*

Born: Dennis Lawson, 1947, actor
Event: The first performance of the musical, *Hair*, in London, 1968

THURSDAY 28th September   St Exuperius

LOVE: Adopt a practical approach to an emotional problem.
LOOT: A good day for salting away your hard-earned cash.
LIFE: Prove what a pillar of strength you can be!
LUCK: ♃

A. M: *P. M:*

Born: Brigitte Bardot, 1934, French film actress
Event: Elizabeth Anderson, the first qualified woman physician & surgeon, 1865

FRIDAY 29th September   St Michael

LOVE: Kind or loving words bring a blush to your cheek!
LOOT: Deals, negotiations or meetings go better than expected.
LIFE: You're even more diplomatic and tactful than usual today!
LUCK: ♃♃♃♃

A. M: *P. M*:

Born: Patricia Hodge, 1946, actress
Event: Richard II abdicates and parliament deposes him, 1399

SATURDAY 30th September   St Jerome

LOVE: Your popularity's on the rise today!
LOOT: Enjoy an away-day or take off on a wee trip.
LIFE: The pace of your life picks up no end now. What a busy bee you
            are!
LUCK: ♃

A. M: *P. M*:

Born: Rula Lenska, 1947, actress
Event: The announcement of the discovery of penicillin, 1928

NOTES:

Sunday 24th November
New Moon in Libra

SEPTEMBER						
S	M	T	W	T	F	S
					1	2
3	4	5	6	7	8	9
10	11	12	13	14	15	16
17	18	19	20	21	22	23
24	25	26	27	28	29	30

SUNDAY 1st October — St Remigius

LOVE: A relative tries to goad you or gets you on the raw.
LOOT: A discussion about cash is the cue for a clash.
LIFE: A difficult day when your temper's always near the surface.
LUCK: U

A. M:

P. M:

Born: Walter Matthau, 1920, US film actor
Event: Henry Ford introduced the Model T,1908

MONDAY 2nd October — St Leodegar

LOVE: One of the clan is a bit too protective for comfort.
LOOT: Buy a loved one a little present or tiny treat.
LIFE: Cherished memories come flooding back today.
LUCK: U

A. M:

P. M:

Born: Anna Ford, 1943, broadcaster
Event: At Twickenham, the first Rugby football match was played, 1909

TUESDAY 3rd October — St Teresa of Lisieux

LOVE: A lovely day for a celebration or party.
LOOT: You're tempted by treats, gifts or little luxuries.
LIFE: Unleash your creative talents on the waiting world!
LUCK: UU

A. M:

P. M:

Born: Sir Michael Hordern, 1911, actor
Event: East Germany and West Germany reunited, 1990

WEDNESDAY 4th October — St Ammon

LOVE: Take care for you're viewing life through rose-coloured specs.
LOOT: Don't commit yourself to anything you can't afford today.
LIFE: If someone leaves your life now, relief will follow grief.
LUCK: UUUU

A. M:

P. M:

Born: Jackie Collins, 1937, author
Event: The first escalator for the public, at Earls Court underground station,1911

THURSDAY 5th October   St Apollinaris of Valence

LOVE: Try not to go it alone today - what a waste that would be!
LOOT: An ideal day for buying and selling. You wheeler dealer, you!
LIFE: A domestic or family worry is starting to sort itself out.
LUCK: ☋☋☋☋

A. M: *P. M*:

Born: Bob Geldof, 1954, rock singer
Event: Unemployed shipyard workers walked to London from Jarrow, 1936

FRIDAY 6th October   St Bruno

LOVE: One of the clan returns to the fold now.
LOOT: A good day to go over accounts or facts and figures.
LIFE: You're a real asset to have around today!
LUCK: ☋☋☋☋

A. M: *P. M*:

Born: Melvyn Bragg, 1939, writer/TV presenter
Event: First talking feature film, *The Jazz Singer,* was shown in New York, 1927

SATURDAY 7th October   St Artaldus

LOVE: Domestic dealings make you feel frayed round the edges.
LOOT: A relative tries to talk you into a wacky or way-out idea.
LIFE: You need to look to the future now and put the past behind you.
LUCK: ☋

A. M: *P. M*:

Born: Desmond TuTu, archbishop of Cape Town, 1931
Event: The Soviet spacecraft, Lunik III, took pictures of the moon, 1959

NOTES:

OCTOBER						
S	M	T	W	T	F	S
1	2	3	4	5	6	7
8	9	10	11	12	13	14
15	16	17	18	19	20	21
22	23	24	25	26	27	28
29	30	31				

SUNDAY 8th October   St Simeon Senex

LOVE: Clear the air with a partner and let them know what's what.
LOOT: If you've been taken for granted lately then put your foot down now.
LIFE: You're an ace at compromise, so you'll excel in the coming fortnight.
LUCK: ᴜᴜᴜᴜ

A. M: *P. M*:

Born: Albert Roux, 1935, chef/restaurateur
Event: The opening of the Post Office Tower in London, 1965

MONDAY 9th October   St Demetrius

LOVE: Your emotions have the upper hand today.
LOOT: Try to be tactful about a partner's strange purchases or taste!
LIFE: Being with dear ones teaches you a lot about yourself now.
LUCK: ᴜ

A. M: *P. M*:

Born: John Lennon, 1940, former Beatle
Event : The first petrol-driven bus started operating in London, 1899

TUESDAY 10th October   St Francis Borgia

LOVE: Your powers of attraction are stronger than ever now!
LOOT: The month ahead is great for investing in luxuries.
LIFE: The needs of loved ones are of paramount importance to you.
LUCK: ᴜ

A. M: *P. M*:

Born: Charles Dance, 1946, actor
Event: Sir John Betjeman appointed Poet Laureate, 1972

WEDNESDAY 11th October   St Atticus

LOVE: Arrange a little surprise or treat for someone who deserves it.
LOOT: Add some glamour or sparkle to your abode.
LIFE: Don't expect everything to go according to plan today.
LUCK: ᴜ

A. M: *P. M*:

Born: Dawn French, 1957, actress/comedienne
Event: Peter the Great became Tsar of Russia, 1669

THURSDAY 12th October   St Wilfrid

LOVE: You take to someone today like a duck to water.
LOOT: How about arranging an outing for the weekend ahead?
LIFE: You're fascinated by all things mystical and spiritual.
LUCK: ᑌᑌᑌ

A. M: *P. M*:

Born: Angela Rippon, 1944, TV presenter
Event: The first Morris Minor was produced, 1948

FRIDAY 13th October   St Edward the Confessor

LOVE: Phew! Keep a wide berth of a certain someone.
LOOT: You get a nasty reminder about a big bill or debt.
LIFE: Try to keep authority figures sweet if possible.
LUCK: ᑌ

A. M: *P. M*:

Born: Paul Simon, 1941, singer/songwriter
Event: George Washington laid the foundation stone of the White House, 1792

SATURDAY 14th October   St Callistus I

LOVE: Recent difficult dealings sort themselves out from today.
LOOT: Expect to hear good news any day now.
LIFE: With communications back on course you're all set for success!
LUCK: ᑌᑌᑌ

A. M: *P. M*:

Born: Roger Moore, 1927, film actor
Event: The Battle of Hastings, 1066

NOTES:

Sunday 8th October
Full Moon in Aries

		OCTOBER				
S	M	T	W	T	F	S
1	2	3	4	5	6	7
8	9	10	11	12	13	14
15	16	17	18	19	20	21
22	23	24	25	26	27	28
29	30	31				

SUNDAY 15th October   St Lucian

LOVE: Make a fuss of someone who's lonely or unhappy.
LOOT: You're feeling generous with love and loot today.
LIFE: Given the choice, you'll opt for pleasure rather than work now.
LUCK: ∪∪

A. M: *P. M:*

Born: Sir Pelham Grenville Wodehouse, 1881, novelist
Event: Mata Hari was executed for espionage, 1917

MONDAY 16th October   St Gall

LOVE: A loved one lets you down or plays football with your heart.
LOOT: Don't be afraid to face the monetary music if needs be.
LIFE: You're feeling lethargic and in need of tender loving care today.
LUCK: ∪

A. M: *P. M:*

Born: Peter Bowles, 1936, actor
Event: Marie Antoinette, Queen of King Louis XVI of France, was executed, 1793

TUESDAY 17th October   St Ignatius of Antioch

LOVE: A friend has some interesting news for you.
LOOT: You're drawn to something for a pet pastime or hobby.
LIFE: Pick a pal's brains about a future scheme or dream.
LUCK: ∪∪

A. M: *P. M:*

Born: Rita Hayworth, 1918, US film actress
Event: Napoleon arrived on the island of St Helena to begin his exile, 1815

WEDNESDAY 18th October   St Luke

LOVE: Social settings see you sparkle and shine.
LOOT: You'll spot something that's beautiful or luxurious.
LIFE: Super for enlisting the support of influential folk.
LUCK: ∪∪

A. M: *P. M:*

Born: Martina Navratilova, 1956, tennis champion
Event: Alaska became officially part of the USA, 1866

THURSDAY 19th October — St Aquilinus of Evreux

LOVE: A loved one acts as if they own you body and soul.
LOOT: Beware of using money as a weapon over someone today.
LIFE: Take care when dealing with folk who are envious or embittered.
LUCK: U

A. M:

P. M:

Born: John Le Carré, 1931, novelist
Event: Lord Cornwallis surrendered, ending the American War of Independence, 1781

FRIDAY 20th October — St Acca

LOVE: One of the clan is defiant, reactionary or cranky today.
LOOT: Money matters connected with home or family go haywire.
LIFE: The pace of your life speeds up no end in the next six weeks.
LUCK: U

A. M:

P. M:

Born: Sir Christopher Wren, 1632, mathematician/architect
Event: The Fascist leader, Benito Mussolini, seized power in Italy, 1922

SATURDAY 21st October — St Hilarion

LOVE: Try to make the best of whatever happens today.
LOOT: Prepare for a surprise about a domestic expense.
LIFE: Someone can't tell the difference between fact and fiction.
LUCK: U

A. M:

P. M:

Born: Dizzy Gillespie, 1917, jazz trumpeter
Event: Admiral Lord Nelson was killed at Trafalgar, 1805

NOTES:

OCTOBER

S	M	T	W	T	F	S
1	*2*	*3*	*4*	*5*	*6*	*7*
8	*9*	*10*	*11*	*12*	*13*	*14*
15	*16*	*17*	*18*	*19*	*20*	*21*
22	*23*	*24*	*25*	*26*	*27*	*28*
29	*30*	*31*				

OCTOBER 1995

SUNDAY 22nd October   St Abercius

LOVE: Your mind and emotions act with one accord today.
LOOT: Try to avoid hasty decisions or impulse buys.
LIFE: A day full of trivia and little incidents.
LUCK: ꙫꙫ

A. M: *P. M*:

Born: Catherine Deneuve, 1943, French film actress
Event: A hurricane killed more that 2000 people when it hit Haiti, 1935

MONDAY 23rd October   St John of Capistrano

LOVE: Someone plays an important role in your life from today.
LOOT: It's a great month for making big investments.
LIFE: Think long and hard about your priorities in life.
LUCK: ꙫꙫꙫ

A. M: *P. M*:

Born: Anita Roddick, 1942, The Body Shop proprietor
Event: The Battle of Edgehill ended with both parties claiming victory, 1642

TUESDAY 24th October   St Anthony Claret

LOVE: Your emotions are deepening, but steer clear of jealousy.
LOOT: Pecuniary prudence will improve your future prospects no end.
LIFE: There are big changes on the way in what matters most to you.
LUCK: ꙫꙫ

A. M: *P. M*:

Born: Sir Robin Day, 1923, TV presenter
Event: Notre Dame Cathedral, Chartres, was consecrated, 1260

WEDNESDAY 25th October   St Crispin & St Crispinian

LOVE: You're able to accept loved ones as they are now.
LOOT: Negotiations and bargain-striking couldn't be better.
LIFE: Off for a job interview? You're a very impressive proposition!
LUCK: ꙫꙫꙫꙫ

A. M: *P. M*:

Born: Helen Reddy, 1942, singer
Event: The English army, led by Henry V, defeated the French at Agincourt, 1415

THURSDAY 26th October   St Demetrius

LOVE: A loved one gets the green-eyed monster. Look out!
LOOT: Money matters could easily cause trouble today.
LIFE: Someone's being unreasonable or plain bloody-minded.
LUCK: ☡

A. M: *P. M:*

Born: Bob Hoskins, 1942, actor
Event: The gunfight at the OK Corral at Tombstone Arizona, 1881

FRIDAY 27th October   St Frumentius of Ethiopia

LOVE: A letter, phone call or visit really makes your day.
LOOT: Great for visiting places near or far.
LIFE: Folk are easy-going, benevolent and good-humoured today.
LUCK: ☡

A. M: *P. M:*

Born: Dylan Thomas, 1914, Welsh Poet
Event: The New York Subway opened, 1904

SATURDAY 28th October   St Firmilian

LOVE: You'll gladly tend to the needs of loved ones today.
LOOT: A super day for buying someone a special treat.
LIFE: You'll get a glimpse of your true priorities in life now.
LUCK: ☡☡

A. M: *P. M:*

Born: Carl Davis, 1936, composer/conductor
Event: A world slump began with the collapse of the New York Stock Exchange, 1929

NOTES:

Tuesday 24th October
Eclipsed New Moon in Scorpio

OCTOBER						
S	M	T	W	T	F	S
1	2	3	4	5	6	7
8	9	10	11	12	13	14
15	16	17	18	19	20	21
22	23	24	25	26	27	28
29	30	31				

SUNDAY 29th October   St Colman of Kilmacduagh

LOVE: One of the clan sulks or maintains a stony silence.
LOOT: Discussions about cash leave a lot to be desired.
LIFE: Someone is too defensive for words today.
LUCK: ♡♡

A. M: P. M:

Born: Michael Jayston, 1935, actor
Event: Sir Walter Raleigh was executed at Westminster, 1618

MONDAY 30th October   St Serapion of Antioch

LOVE: You've got a bone to pick with a loved one!
LOOT: Money matters are like a red rag to a bull for you today.
LIFE: You don't have the patience for fiddly or detailed pursuits now.
LUCK: ♡

A. M: P. M:

Born: Henry Winkler, 1945, US actor
Even: Orson Welles' play, *The War of the Worlds*, was broadcast, 1938

TUESDAY 31st October   St Wolfgang

LOVE: A loved one's too set in their ways for you today.
LOOT: Why not do something you've always fancied?
LIFE: Forget your usual routine and weave some magic into your life.
LUCK: ♡♡

A. M: P. M:

Born: Dick Francis, 1920, novelist
Event: The Battle of Britain ended, 1940

WEDNESDAY 1st November   All Saints

LOVE: Someone's kind words thrill you to the core!
LOOT: Good for asking the family about future plans.
LIFE: You'll hear interesting or heart-warming snippets from the past.
LUCK: ♡♡

A. M: P. M:

Born: Nigel Dempster, 1941, Journalist
Event: The M1 motorway was opened, 1959

THURSDAY *2nd November* — St Eustace

LOVE: You long to shake up a loved one who's living in the past.
LOOT: You could have a controversial idea about your abode.
LIFE: Expect little upsets and interruptions all day long.
LUCK: U

A. M: *P. M:*

Born: Burt Lancaster, 1913, US film actor
Event: *The Sunday Express* published the first crossword puzzle, 1924

FRIDAY *3rd November* — St Hubert

LOVE: A special someone tries to bind you to them with hoops of steel.
LOOT: Beware of believing that you can buy a loved one's affections.
LIFE: Step into the social scene, starting today!
LUCK: U

A. M: *P. M:*

Born: Lulu, 1948, singer
Event: An Act was passed making the monarch head of the English Church, 1534

SATURDAY *4th November* — St Charles Borromeo

LOVE: This month is perfect for discussing your needs with dear ones.
LOOT: Cash in on the money-making ideas you have, starting today.
LIFE: Ponder long and hard about your true values in life.
LUCK: UU

A. M: *P. M:*

Born: Loretta Swit, 1944, US Actress
Event: Howard Carter & Lord Carnarvon discovered the Tutankhamun, 1922

NOTES:

NOVEMBER						
S	M	T	W	T	F	S
			1	2	3	4
5	6	7	8	9	10	11
12	13	14	15	16	17	18
19	20	21	22	23	24	25
26	27	28	29	30		

NOVEMBER 1995

SUNDAY 5th November — St Elizabeth

LOVE: A dear one's dreary demeanour gives you a very short fuse.
LOOT: You're determined to do the opposite of what folk tell you today.
LIFE: Plagued by a bad habit? Then give it a rocket today!
LUCK: ♘♘♘♘

A. M: P. M:

Born: Vivien Leigh, 1913, actress
Event: The title, "King of France", was abandoned by the British sovereign,

MONDAY 6th November — St Illtyd

LOVE: A loved one's outspoken behaviour arouses your indignation.
LOOT: Is someone playing fast and loose with a joint account?
LIFE: Try to keep problems in perspective today.
LUCK: ♘

A. M: P. M:

Born: Nigel Havers, 1949, actor
Event: Mexico declared her Independence, 1813

TUESDAY 7th November — St Willibrord

LOVE: Someone's jealousy or envy needs to be nipped in the bud.
LOOT: Get to grips with official money matters in the coming fortnight.
LIFE: You're developing a more serious and profound approach to life.
LUCK: ♘

A. M: P. M:

Born: Jean Shrimpton, 1942, former model
Event: The last public hanging in England at Tyburn, 1783

WEDNESDAY 8th November — St Willehad

LOVE: You're touched by a loved one's problem or dilemma.
LOOT: Invite the clan round for a meal or cosy chat.
LIFE: You'll absorb the moods of others like a sponge, so take care.
LUCK: ♘

A. M: P. M:

Born: Bram Stoker, 1847, author of *Dracula*
Event: X-rays were discovered by Wilhelm Rontgen, 1895

THURSDAY 9th November — St Simeon Metaphrastes

LOVE: Someone jumps to the wrong conclusion.
LOOT: A neighbour or everyday contact kicks up a rumpus.
LIFE: You're sick and tired of a partner's attitude towards you.
LUCK: ♘♘

A. M: P. M:

Born: Katherine Hepburn, 1909, US actress
Event: In Britain, the death penalty for murder was abolished, 1965

FRIDAY 10th November — St Justus

LOVE: An everyday encounter could transform your life now!
LOOT: The more painstaking you are over cash today, the better.
LIFE: It's time to review and revise your daily routine.
LUCK: ♘♘

A. M: P. M:

Born: Richard Burton, 1935, actor
Event: An airmail service started between London and Paris, 1919

SATURDAY 11th November — St Martin of Tours

LOVE: Are there people in your life who no longer fit into it?
LOOT: You need to review your daily outgoings, but do it slowly.
LIFE: Cut out any situations or circumstances that are holding you back.
LUCK: ♘♘

A. M: P. M:

Born: June Whitfield,1925, actress
Event: The World War I armistice was signed between the Allies & Germany, 1918

NOTES:

Tuesday 7th November
Full Moon in Taurus

NOVEMBER						
S	M	T	W	T	F	S
			1	2	3	4
5	6	7	8	9	10	11
12	13	14	15	16	17	18
19	20	21	22	23	24	25
26	27	28	29	30		

SUNDAY 12th November   St Benedict

LOVE: You realise the importance someone has for you today.
LOOT: Good for buying things that enhance your ego or appearance.
LIFE: You'll bask in a loved one's reflected glory now.
LUCK: ☾☾☾

A. M: *P. M:*

Born: Princess Grace of Monaco (Grace Kelly), 1929
Event: The bodies of Captain Scott and companions were found in Antarctica, 1912

MONDAY 13th November   St Abbo

LOVE: A loved one tries to put you down or demoralise you.
LOOT: Not a good time for signing contracts or agreements.
LIFE: Someone may try to restrict you or stand in your way.
LUCK: ☾☾

A. M: *P. M:*

Born: Robert Louis Stevenson, 1850, writer/traveller
Event: Texas declared its Independence from Mexico, 1835

TUESDAY 14th November   St Dubricius

LOVE: If you want to make a big impression then make a big effort!
LOOT: You could be careless over cash concerns now.
LIFE: Someone damns an idea with faint praise.
LUCK: ☾

A. M: *P. M:*

Born: HRH the Prince of Wales, 1948
Event: Colour television transmissions began in Britain, 1969

WEDNESDAY 15th November   St Albert the Great

LOVE: Someone needs a sympathetic shoulder to cry on.
LOOT: Go through what you did yesterday and rectify any mistakes.
LIFE: You're practical, pragmatic and impressive!
LUCK: ☾☾☾☾

A. M: *P. M:*

Born: Sam Waterston, 1940, US actor
Event: The shorthand system of Isaac Pitman was published, 1837

THURSDAY 16th November   St Edmund of Abingdon

LOVE: You're fascinated by the breadth of someone's knowledge.
LOOT: It's a super day for buying things that boost your brainpower.
LIFE: Take the broad view in all your dealings today.
LUCK: ☾☾☾☾

A. M: *P. M*:

Born: Frank Bruno, 1961, boxer
Event: The formal opening of the first Westminster Bridge, 1750

FRIDAY 17th November   St Elizabeth of Hungary

LOVE: Are your relationships bringing you what you want and need?
LOOT: You're ace at devising budgets and spending plans today.
LIFE: Try to spend some time all by yourself now.
LUCK: ☾☾☾☾

A. M: *P. M*:

Born: Peter Cook, 1937, writer/entertainer
Event: Elizabeth I acceded to the English throne, 1558

SATURDAY 18th November   St Odo

LOVE: You'll know exactly what's wrong with a loved one.
LOOT: Think about financial plans but don't put them into action yet.
LIFE: It's a good day to add personal touches to your abode.
LUCK: ☾☾

A. M: *P. M*:

Born: David Hemmings, 1941, actor/director
Event: The first Mickey Mouse cartoon was screened, 1928

NOTES:

NOVEMBER						
S	M	T	W	T	F	S
			1	2	3	4
5	6	7	8	9	10	11
12	13	14	15	16	17	18
19	20	21	22	23	24	25
26	27	28	29	30		

NOVEMBER 1995

SUNDAY 19th November   St Mechthild

LOVE: Someone you meet showers blessings on you today.
LOOT: If you're off to the shops then you'll come back laden!
LIFE: Satisfy your craving for company with convivial folk.
LUCK: ○○○○○

A. M: P. M:

Born: Jodie Foster, 1963, US actress
Event: President Lincoln delivered his Gettysburg address, 1863

MONDAY 20th November   St Edmund the Martyr

LOVE: You discover a new side to someone you know very well.
LOOT: Bored with your abode? Then make some alterations now!
LIFE: How about planning a family party or gathering?
LUCK: ○○

A. M: P. M:

Born: Robert Kennedy, 1925, US politician
Event: Princess Elizabeth married the Duke of Edinburgh, 1947

TUESDAY 21st November   St Gelasius

LOVE: A loved one's idea or suggestion knocks you for six!
LOOT: Get ready for a brainwave about how to transform your home!
LIFE: Have another stab at your diet or health regime.
LUCK: ○○

A. M: P. M:

Born: Goldie Hawn, 1945, US film actress
Event: First hot-air balloon flight was made by the Montgolfier brothers, 1783

WEDNESDAY 22nd November   St Cecillia

LOVE: The scales fall from your eyes now about a certain someone.
LOOT: Fancy starting a nice nestegg for a golden future?
LIFE: Ponder on what really matters to you in life.
LUCK: ○○○

A. M: P. M:

Born: Boris Becker, 1967, tennis champion
Event: President Kennedy was assassinated at Dallas, Texas, 1963

THURSDAY 23rd November St Amphilochius

LOVE: Daily encounters are imbued with intensity this week.
LOOT: Something finally goes on the blink or gives up the ghost.
LIFE: A conversation or communication has powerful results.
LUCK: UUU

A. M: *P. M:*

Born: Diana Quick, 1946, actress
Event: The first pillar box was built at St Helier, Jersey, 1852

FRIDAY 24th November St Chrysogonus

LOVE: Flirtatious, vivacious and charming. Who could that be but you?
LOOT: Off to the shops? You'll want to spend, spend, spend!
LIFE: Don your best togs and head for the nearest gathering!
LUCK: UUUU

A. M: *P. M:*

Born: Billy Connolly, 1942, comedian
Event: Charles Darwin's *Origin of Species* was published, 1859

SATURDAY 25th November St Clement I

LOVE: A loved one proves that they're a pillar of strength.
LOOT: Work out budgets or spending plans today.
LIFE: A family problem calls for careful handling.
LUCK: U

A. M: *P. M:*

Born: Francis Durbridge, 1912, author/playwright
Event: *The Mousetrap*, by Agatha Christie, opened in London, 1952

NOTES:

Wednesday 22nd November
New Moon in Scorpio

NOVEMBER

S	M	T	W	T	F	S
			1	*2*	*3*	*4*
5	*6*	*7*	*8*	*9*	*10*	*11*
12	*13*	*14*	*15*	*16*	*17*	*18*
19	*20*	*21*	*22*	*23*	*24*	*25*
26	*27*	*28*	*29*	*30*		

SUNDAY 26th November — St Siricius

LOVE: You'll make a new friend or acquaintance today.
LOOT: Spend a little cash on enjoying yourself!
LIFE: The folk in your life are chatty, convivial and kind now.
LUCK: ʊʊ

A. M: *P. M*:

Born: Tina Turner, 1938, US rock singer
Event: In England 8,000 people were killed during the Great Storm, 1703

MONDAY 27th November — St Virgil

LOVE: Home is where your heart and happiness lie in the coming month.
LOOT: It's a super time for making your nest extra cosy and attractive.
LIFE: Surround yourself with familiar faces and places in the month
        ahead.
LUCK: ʊʊ

A. M: *P. M*:

Born: Ernie Wise, 1925, comedian
Event: The first two women joined the police force at Grantham, 1914

TUESDAY 28th November — St James

LOVE: Life takes on extra meaning today, thanks to a certain someone.
LOOT: Buy things that increase the comfort in your life.
LIFE: Being at home with loved ones is just what the doctor ordered!
LUCK: ʊʊʊʊ

A. M: *P. M*:

Born: Nancy Mitford, 1904, novelist/biographer
Event: Albania proclaimed Independence from Turkey, 1912

WEDNESDAY 29th November — St Cuthbert Mayne

LOVE: Mind your Ps and Qs unless you want to start a slanging match.
LOOT: Try to sort out money muddles without raising cain.
LIFE: A neighbour, colleague or close pal makes you see red.
LUCK: ʊ

A. M: *P. M*:

Born: Busby Berkeley, 1895, film director/choreographer
Event: Yugoslavia became the Federal People's Republic, 1945

THURSDAY 30th November — St Andrew

LOVE: Try to compromise from today or there'll be conflicts galore.
LOOT: You'll put your heart and soul into making your abode perfect now.
LIFE: Go carefully in the next month or folk may oppose you for no apparent reason.
LUCK: ὑὑὑὑ

A. M: P. M:

Born: Sir Winston Churchill, 1874
Event: Oscar Wilde, the playwright, died in Paris, 1900

FRIDAY 1st December — St Eligius

LOVE: You're even more tactful and diplomatic than usual today!
LOOT: Written your Christmas card list yet? Then get cracking now!
LIFE: Pour harmonious oil on any troubled waters.
LUCK: ὑὑ

A. M: P. M:

Born: Woody Allen, 1935, US film actor/writer/director
Event: Lady Nancy Astor, first woman MP, took her in the seat in the House of Commons

SATURDAY 2nd December — St Chromatius

LOVE: Is a loved one telling you the whole truth or just part of it?
LOOT: Make your intentions very plain today or there'll be a muddle.
LIFE: Old habits die hard today, so go carefully.
LUCK: ὑὑὑὑ

A. M: P. M:

Born: Maria Callas, 1923, opera singer
Event: Pope Pius VII crowned Napoleon Emperor in Paris, 1804

NOTES:

DECEMBER						
S	M	T	W	T	F	S
				1	2	3
4	5	6	7	8	9	10
11	12	13	14	15	16	17
18	19	20	21	22	23	24
25	26	27	28	29	30	31

SUNDAY 3rd December — St Francis Xavier

LOVE: Convert your fond feelings into ardent actions!
LOOT: If you disagree over a shared affair then say so today.
LIFE: You're eager to start a home project but will you finish it?
LUCK: U

A. M: P. M:

Born: Paul Nicholas, 1945, actor/singer
Event: First heart transplant performed by Dr Christian Barnard in South Africa, 1967

MONDAY 4th December — St Barbara

LOVE: Someone's off-the-cuff comments result in a crestfallen you.
LOOT: Go through paperwork on your ownsome if you can.
LIFE: You're ace at concentrating but bad at communicating today.
LUCK: U

A. M: P. M:

Born: Jeff Bridges, 1949, US film actor
Event: William Pitt the Younger introduced income tax, 1798

TUESDAY 5th December — St Clement of Alexandria

LOVE: Ginger up a long-term relationship by adding a little spice.
LOOT: Want to give your home a new look before the festivities? Then start now!
LIFE: You'll see an old problem in a radical new light today.
LUCK: U

A. M: P. M:

Born: Walt Disney, 1901
Event: The first British woman priest was ordained in New Jersey, USA, 1981

WEDNESDAY 6th December — St Nicholas

LOVE: Get out and about if you're looking for someone to love.
LOOT: It's a super time to improve your mode of transport.
LIFE: Is your diary blank for December? Then fill up the pages pronto!
LUCK: UUUU

A. M: P. M:

Born: Dave Brubeck, 1920, US Jazz musician
Event: In America, Gerald Ford was sworn in as vice-president, 1973

THURSDAY *7th December*   St Ambrose

LOVE: Someone teaches you a lesson you'll never forget now.
LOOT: Held back by lack of skills? Then further your education from today.
LIFE: Resolve a question of conscience as honestly and fairly as possible.
LUCK: ☾☾☾☾

A. M: *P. M*:

Born: Ellen Burstyn, 1932, US actress
Event: An imperial edict was issued that all Chinese had to cut off their pigtails, 1911

FRIDAY *8th December*   St Patapius

LOVE: Make an effort to work out what makes someone tick.
LOOT: The perfect day for discussions, negotiations and deals.
LIFE: You're fair but firm in all your dealings today.
LUCK: ☾☾☾☾

A. M: *P. M*:

Born: Maximilian Schell, 1930, German actor
Event: The Immaculate Conception was promulgated by Pope Pius IX, 1854

SATURDAY *9th December*   St Budoc

LOVE: Someone turns on the tears or causes a scene.
LOOT: Stick faithfully to your list if you're off to the shops!
LIFE: A day when feelings run high, though out of bad will come good.
LUCK: ☾

A. M: *P. M*:

Born: Dame Judi Dench, 1934, actress
Event: Lech Walesa was elected president of Poland, 1990

NOTES:

Thursday 7th December
Full Moon in Gemini

DECEMBER						
S	M	T	W	T	F	S
					1	2	3
4	5	6	7	8	9	10
11	12	13	14	15	16	17
18	19	20	21	22	23	24
25	26	27	28	29	30	31

SUNDAY 10th December   St Miltiades

LOVE: Someone's frosty and frigid air chills you to the bone.
LOOT: Money matters plunge you into doom and gloom now.
LIFE: You're forced to choose between duty and pleasure today.
LUCK: ☉

A. M: P. M:

Born: Kenneth Branagh, 1960, actor/director
Event: Abdication of King Edward VIII, 1936

MONDAY 11th December   St Damasus

LOVE: It's a super month for talking honestly about what's in your heart.
LOOT: Got plans for your home or family? Then discuss them with the clan.
LIFE: Past events have an important bearing on what happens now.
LUCK: ☉

A. M: P. M:

Born: Sir Kenneth MacMillan, 1929, choreographer
Event: King George VI acceded to the throne, 1936

TUESDAY 12th December   St Alexander

LOVE: One of the clan really relies on you today.
LOOT: Continue discussions where you left them yesterday or take them further.
LIFE: A most auspicious day for strengthening the roots of your world.
LUCK: ☉☉☉☉

A. M: P. M:

Born: Kenneth Cranham, 1994, actor
Event: Independence of Kenya, 1963, became a Republic on this day in 1964

WEDNESDAY 13th December   St Lucy

LOVE: Declare your devotion or reveal the state of your heart.
LOOT: Someone's pecuniary plight earns an instant response from you.
LIFE: How about having an impromptu gathering of the clan?
LUCK: ☉

A. M: P. M:

Born: Robert Lindsay, 1949, actor
Event: The first sound movie was shown by Dr Lee De Forest in America, 1923

THURSDAY 14th December St John of the Cross

LOVE: You can't pussyfoot around a sensitive issue any longer!
LOOT: A good day to do some DIY but don't start things you can't finish.
LIFE: Cash in on today's forceful and forthright mood.
LUCK: U

A. M: *P. M:*

Born: Barbara Leigh-Hunt, 1935, actress
Event: British women voted for the first time at the General Election, 1918

FRIDAY 15th December St Mary di Rosa

LOVE: A loved one's just waiting for a chance to let off steam.
LOOT: Something you wanted to cover up rises to the surface.
LIFE: Folk are temperamental, tart, gruff or grumpy today.
LUCK: U

A. M: *P. M:*

Born: Edna O'Brien, 1936, Irish novelist
Event: The premiere of, *Gone with the Wind,* was held at Atlanta, Georgia, 1939

SATURDAY 16th December St Eusebius

LOVE: How dare they! A close companion leaves you lost for words.
LOOT: Family plans or possessions cause a clash in the clan.
LIFE: You're feeling defensive and huffy today, so proceed with caution.
LUCK: U

A. M: *P. M:*

Born: Liv Ullmann, 1938, actress
Event: The opening of the production of the musical, *Me and My Girl*, 1937

NOTES:

DECEMBER

S	M	T	W	T	F	S
				1	*2*	*3*
4	*5*	*6*	*7*	*8*	*9*	*10*
11	*12*	*13*	*14*	*15*	*16*	*17*
18	*19*	*20*	*21*	*22*	*23*	*24*
25	*26*	*27*	*28*	*29*	*30*	*31*

SUNDAY 17th December — St Begga

LOVE: An indefinable something is missing when you're with a dear one.
LOOT: Try to make your own decisions and don't let others persuade you.
LIFE: Iced the cake yet? Then let your imagination run riot over it!
LUCK: ♻♻♻♻

A. M: P. M:

Born: Christopher Cazenove, 1945, actor
Event: Pierre Auguste Renoir, the French Impressionist, died, 1919

MONDAY 18th December — St Frumentius

LOVE: Someone's suggestion or invitation gets you buzzing with excitement.
LOOT: Boodle burns a hole in your pocket but you don't care!
LIFE: A wonderful day for proving that you're the star of the social scene.
LUCK: ♻♻♻♻

A. M: P. M:

Born: Keith Richards, 1943, Rolling Stone guitarist
Event: The sound barrier was broken on land by Stanley Barrett in California, 1979

TUESDAY 19th December — St Anastasius I of Antioch

LOVE: A loved one makes your world go round today.
LOOT: How about treating yourself to some of life's little luxuries?
LIFE: Sort out a family problem so everyone's happy again.
LUCK: ♻

A. M: P. M:

Born: Sir Ralph Richardson, 1902, actor
Event: Ted Hughes was appointed Poet Laureate, 1984

WEDNESDAY 20th December — St Ignatius of Antioch

LOVE: If a relationship is getting dull then stir it up today!
LOOT: Buy something with a difference for your wee nest.
LIFE: Prepare for exciting disruptions and interruptions to your day.
LUCK: ♻

A. M: P. M:

Born: Jenny Agutter, 1952, actress
Event: The State of Texas became part of the United States, 1845

THURSDAY 21st December   St Peter Canisius

LOVE: It's a fantastic month for taking a love affair one step further!
LOOT: Fancy a new image? Then start as you mean to go on!
LIFE: You'll be walking in a winter wonderland from today.
LUCK: ʊʊʊʊ

A. M: *P. M:*

Born: Frank Zappa, 1940, rock musician
Event: Apollo 8 was launched, taking man to the moon for the first time, 1969

FRIDAY 22nd December   St Anastasia

LOVE: Let bygones be bygones - it's the future that counts.
LOOT: Think seriously about improving or extending your abode or
        family.
LIFE: Involve yourself more in your own community or neighbourhood.
LUCK: ʊʊ

A. M: *P. M:*

Born: Patricia Hayes, 1909, actress
Event: Lincoln's Inn Theatre staged the first pantomime in England, 1716

SATURDAY 23rd December   St John of Kanty

LOVE: A loving liaison is transformed for the better today.
LOOT: Great for snapping up last-minute gifts or decorations.
LIFE: A party or get-together is the start of a wonderful Christmas.
LUCK: ʊʊ

A. M: *P. M:*

Born: Maurice Denham, 1909, actor
Event: A form of horse-drawn cab was patented by Joseph Hansom, 1834

NOTES:

Friday 22nd December
New Moon in Sagittarius

DECEMBER						
S	M	T	W	T	F	S
				1	2	3
4	5	6	7	8	9	10
11	12	13	14	15	16	17
18	19	20	21	22	23	24
25	26	27	28	29	30	31

SUNDAY 24th December — St Adela

LOVE: You're touched by memories of Christmas past.
LOOT: An unexpected expense puts you in a panic.
LIFE: Make time to put your feet up or you'll be fit for nowt tomorrow.
LUCK: U

A. M:

P. M:

Born: Ava Gardner, 1922, US film actress
Event: The first performance of Giuseppe Verdi's opera, *Aida,* at Cairo, 1871

MONDAY 25th December Christmas Day — St Alburga

LOVE: Use some festive cheer to lighten up someone's serious mood.
LOOT: Someone makes you the offer you've been waiting for.
LIFE: Immerse yourself in the Christmas spirit. Wassail!
LUCK: UUUU

A. M:

P. M:

Born: Humphrey Bogart, 1899, actor
Event: Vaclav Havel was elected president of Czechoslovakia, 1989

TUESDAY 26th December — St Stephen

LOVE: You're suddenly overcome by memories of Christmas past.
LOOT: Settle up with one of the clan over who owes what to whom.
LIFE: Surround yourself with familiar faces and places.
LUCK: U

A. M:

P. M:

Born: Richard Widmark, 1914, US film actor
Event: Fidel Castro landed in Cuba, 1956

WEDNESDAY 27th December — St John

LOVE: Go carefully, for a loved one is feeling very vulnerable today.
LOOT: How about snapping up some household bargains in the sales?
LIFE: Try to steer clear of negative folk or they'll make you miserable.
LUCK: U

A. M:

P. M:

Born: Marlene Dietrich, 1901, film actress
Event: The first performance of J M Barrie's play, *Peter Pan*, London, 1904

THURSDAY 28th December   St Anthony of Lerins

LOVE: One of the clan tells tales or gives completely the wrong
          impression.
LOOT: Try not to get carried away if heading for the sales!
LIFE: It's a marvellous day for titivating or redecorating your dwelling.
LUCK: ꙨꙨꙨ

A. M: *P. M:*

Born: Dame Maggie Smith, 1934, actress
Event: The world's first public film show in Paris, 1895

FRIDAY 29th December   St Thomas à Becket

LOVE: Family ties enfold you in a blanket of love and affection now.
          Lovely!
LOOT: A relative needs some financial help or advice, so see what you can
          do.
LIFE: Home and hearth are where your heart is this month.
LUCK: Ꙩ

A. M: *P. M:*
Born: Jon Voight, 1938, US film actor
Event: Radio Luxembourg started broadcasting, 1930

SATURDAY 30th December   St Anysia

LOVE: A partner or relative is hot under the collar - and how!
LOOT: Family matters or domestic ideas raise a right old rumpus.
LIFE: Batten down the hatches - someone's out for your blood!
LUCK: ꙨꙨꙨꙨ

A. M: *P. M:*

Born: Tracy Ullman, 1959, actress/comedienne
Event: King Michael of Romania abdicated, 1947

NOTES:

DECEMBER						
S	M	T	W	T	F	S
					1	2	3
4	5	6	7	8	9	10
11	12	13	14	15	16	17
18	19	20	21	22	23	24
25	26	27	28	29	30	31

SUNDAY 31st December   St Sylvester

LOVE: You'll reach an important decision about a dear one today.
LOOT: Iron out domestic or official matters ready for a new start in 1996.
LIFE: Ponder carefully on what you want from life and how to get it.
LUCK: ℧

A. M: *P. M*:

Born: Sir Anthony Hopkins, 1937, actor
Event: The chimes of Big Ben were broadcast by the BBC for the first time, 1923

NOTES: